D0911291

SOLVING THE
ATLANTIS
MYSTERY

How the mythical island rose out of the Ice Age

MICHAEL HORN

Solving the Atlantis Mystery

How the mythical island rose out of the Ice Age

Michael Horn

Book cover painting by Jon Horn

ISBN: 978-1-66786-828-8

ISBN: 978-1-66786-829-5

To Jill and our companion, Penny

CONTENTS

INTRODUCTION

What if it was shown that Atlantis was once a real place—not just a myth? That would be a headline event. Just imagine how that would change what we think about the history of Western civilization. It would also add a new dimension to the understanding of geology. It would clearly be the unraveling of the mystery behind one of the greatest legends of all time.

This book explores two levels of novel discovery to unravel the mystery of Atlantis. First, it discusses the hypothesis that a large, geologically unstable landmass existed and may in the future reappear in the middle of the Atlantic Ocean, an island that rises and subsides according to the rhythm of episodically occurring glacial periods. Second, and on a more contemporary level, it asserts that this landmass could fulfill the claim of Plato's Atlantis, the "mythical" island that hosted a civilization prior to the classical Greeks and even before the monumental pyramid-building dynastic Egyptian cultures.

The book explains why it is entirely probable, to a great degree of certainty, that the island of Atlantis, the most enduring myth of Western civilization, was in fact a real place in history. Furthermore, it presents such a strong case for how it first appeared and then disappeared that the most ardent skeptics will have to reexamine their objections and admit that it is entirely likely. The argument presented here will support, beyond a reasonable doubt, Plato's assertions for this large Atlantic island. It also shows how he correctly pinpointed its demise, which coincided with the end of the last ice age.

My interest in the Atlantis myth became entangled with my side interest in geology and the fascinating dynamics of undersea mountain ranges. In the course of my studies of the latter—mid-ocean ridges, as they are referred to in geology—I was led to a book published in 1882 by Ignatius Donnelly, *Atlantis: The Antediluvian World*, that discussed the newly discovered submerged Atlantic Ocean mountain range. Donnelly's book was based on the premise that this undersea mountain range was Atlantis. But because of the primitive understanding of geology of the time, the author was unable to reasonably demonstrate a scientific basis for his hypothesis. Although the book was riddled with geological fallacies, it presented a map of the Atlantic Ocean with the outline of the mid-ocean mountain range that he claimed was Atlantis (see figure 1-I). That image stuck in my mind when I began to realize that the author's supposition was not so far-fetched at all when viewed from a novel perspective.

To develop a reasonable hypothesis of my own, I needed to understand exactly what Plato had originally claimed about Atlantis. What I came to learn was that it was all contained in two of Plato's dialogues, *Timaeus* and *Critias,* as translated by Benjamin Jowett in 1871. Those works portray the Atlantis myth in its entirety. I found that something about Plato's description of Atlantis bore a startling resemblance to what I knew about those mid-ocean ridges, or undersea mountain ranges.

This building interest in what Plato said about Atlantis was at about the time—a period of almost twenty years—when I was an aerospace research scientist at the Northrop Grumman Corporate Research Center, collaborating with other labs in the US government and in academia. I was a principal investigator for research collaborations with institutes such as NASA, Wright-Patterson Air Force Base, and Ames Research Center at Iowa State University, as well as many others. The mission of my lab was the advanced development of new tools for the materials sciences. These research and development efforts took up most of my time and required an inordinate degree of concentration, pushing my interest in Atlantis to the back burner—until now.

Since retiring from the aerospace world, I have been able to redirect my time and efforts back to figuring out this Atlantis mystery. I was once again absorbed by the compelling aspects of this ancient story that also had a strange ring of truth by today's scientific understanding. I was most notably struck by Plato's claims that Atlantis sank nine thousand years before his time—which was exactly at the end of the last ice age.

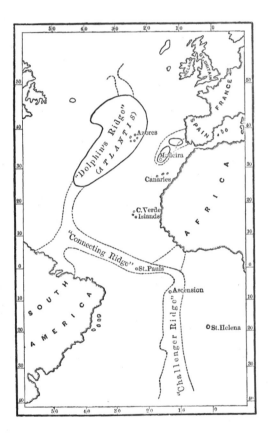

Figure 1-I. *Map in the Donnelly book that claimed to depict the lost continent of Atlantis.*

The ice age seems such a primordial time, and the thought that any civilization could have existed that far back seems almost impossible. But I soon learned that there was at least one civilization in existence then, at a place in Turkey called Gobekli Tepe. Discovered only recently, in 1996, its inhabitants had built large monoliths and stone temple structures, deftly embellished with an assortment of wild animals and birds. Judging by their ability to construct these elaborately carved structures, these people didn't appear to be primitive at all. The peoples of Gobekli Tepe lived in a period known as the Pre-Pottery Neolithic, a time when archaeologists, until only recently, had no idea such a civilization could possibly have existed. Remarkably enough, I came to realize that this post-Pleistocene period in history wasn't the mere coincidence it might at first appear but was, as it turned out, a fundamental clue. The more information I collected from my research, the more pieces of the puzzle unfolded before me.

The time in which Plato places Atlantis was one of dynamic climate change. The last ice age was a period when the sea levels were hundreds of feet lower than they are today. I came to recognize that this was the start of the chain of events that, I believe, once created and then destroyed the legendary island of Atlantis.

Despite gathering all the evidence I have that leads to the inevitable conclusion that there was once a great Atlantic island, there is plenty of room for specialists in the field to produce the sophisticated computer simulations to provide the concrete proof of my hypothesis. Clearly, though, the proof of this novel idea will undo some commonly accepted beliefs surrounding not only geology and oceanography but also paleoanthropology and archaeology. It concerns the incredible things that transpired during the Pleistocene, the most recent age before the one we're in now, which is the Holocene. Currently, archaeologists can see no evidence that Atlantis is any more than a mythical place, inasmuch as there is no collective of supporting fossils or ruins with which to draw anything other than a negative conclusion.

However, the case I present here opens the door for a logical and systematic discussion by all the related scientific disciplines about whether a certain process has been overlooked that might lead to corroborating the ancient existence of the Atlantic island recorded by Plato. This is the first book to offer a complete, science-based, plausible explanation using currently accepted geological models that build the case step by step.

The latest trend in the genre of Atlantis books has been to place it in locations other than the Atlantic Ocean—such as the island of Santorini in the Mediterranean, or England, or Antarctica—for no other reason than those before have been unsuccessful in formulating a satisfactory scientific explanation to show that it existed right where Plato said it did—in the Atlantic Ocean.

Presently, the concept of a sunken island in the Atlantic is at odds with today's conventional geologic view of the Mid-Atlantic Ridge, the geology of which provides no quick or direct answers as to how it would have risen and then sunk to such an enormous degree. Developing a convincing scientifically based theory has eluded investigators up until now. Previously, authors placing Atlantis in the Atlantic skirted the issue of a geological explanation. As a consequence, most authors have chosen to situate Atlantis in other places around the world (see figure 2-I).

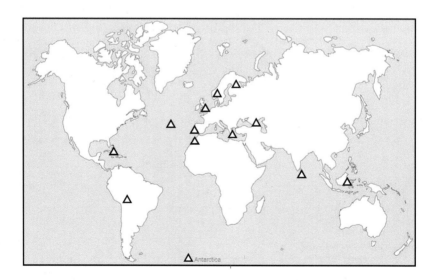

Figure 2-I. Places previous authors and investigators believed Atlantis may have been located.

The theory I propose confronts all the nettlesome issues of Atlantis and explains them, from its rise during the Pleistocene to its sinking at the end of that last ice age.

What I consider a truly exciting aspect of this book is the unequivocal revelation that the Mid-Atlantic Ridge has undergone substantial excursions, above and below sea level, a fact that I've failed to find mentioned in any geological abstracts.

As presented here, the geological mechanisms that play out beneath the Mid-Atlantic Ridge are still poorly understood and open to debate by geologists today. But the enormous geological activity along the ridge is one thing about which all of them can agree. Much more is known about the surface of the ridge than many other parts of the ocean bottom, which has been mapped by several oceanographic surveys. Yet it is said that more is known about the surface of the moon and Mars than about the earth's seafloor!

Nevertheless, without knowing any more than geologists already do about the structure and dynamics of this submerged mid-ocean mountain range, I show through known geological processes that a large extent of the Mid-Atlantic Ridge was above sea level just before the end of the last ice age. I admit that the scenario I propose would not be immediately obvious unless one considers several geological events and phenomena, happening in concert, that up until now might have seemed to be unrelated—which probably explains why it hasn't been noticed before.

The basic hypothesis I propose demonstrates how the redistribution of water over the earth's surface, caused by the formation of the ice age glaciers, led to the unleashing of forces that produced a cascading series of geological events that culminated in the rise and eventual sinking of Atlantis.

The events following the formation of the glaciers and lowered sea levels not only reveal how the Mid-Atlantic Ridge was capable of rising and sinking but also provide the enabling evidence needed to show that

Atlantis could very well have existed where the legend claims it did. It also opens the door to further speculation as to whether humans might have discovered this land and what potential effect, if any, it might have had on cross-pollination between the peoples of Europe/Africa and North America during the Pleistocene.

Although I have prepared some simple mathematical calculations to show to what extent the island likely rose above sea level, this book can be read without having to dally with those back-of-the-envelope calculations. They're only meant for those who have an interest in understanding the extent of my objective reasoning, so don't let them scare you off; the theory can be completely understood without any numbers. But those who are interested will find them a convincing means to establishing to what degree the geologic forces they endeavor to depict were able to create the island of the antediluvian legend.

In returning to a period around ten thousand years in the past, we see how a large landmass such as was described by Plato could have existed when and where he claimed, not in some fanciful location that suits just some of what he said. I believe that the large landmass to which Plato refers is actually where he said it was and that it is the Mid-Atlantic Ridge.

It happens that the margin of the ridge, or the crest of this mountain range, is the convergence point of unimaginable forces and, at once, the divergence of the seafloor itself. It is these forces that were responsible for driving North America away from Eurasia in what is commonly referred to today as continental drift and, technically, the realm of plate tectonics. We've all probably seen the animated illustrations of the continents jammed together as one giant landmass, only to split apart, assiduously sliding along to form the map of the present-day earth.

Only as recently as the 1960s did scientists first discover that the continents were moving as a result of these titanic geological forces. Based on my study of what geologists currently know about the dynamics of the ridge and what I've learned from the geologic research they have already carried out, I believe that a proper explanation can be presented that provides indirect evidence for the past existence of a large island in the Atlantic Ocean: Atlantis.

Furthermore, it's impossible, as I'm writing this, to know exactly how high the Mid-Atlantic Ridge actually poked above the waves, but it becomes clear that this ridge most certainly does move up and down. This becomes immediately understandable with even a casual examination of the bathymetric maps of the Atlantic Ocean, which instantly convey the impression that some extraordinary geologic process is at play under the ridge. But this is not an accepted geological phenomenon, the reason for which appears to be that nobody has put these disparate geophysical aspects together as I have.

This enormous sunken mountain range is above sea level in places such as the Azores but remains largely submerged along the greater part of its extent. The Azores are on an adjacent plateau that is part of a confluence of another very active spreading center. So, it's not like it couldn't have happened, just that nobody has pointed it out as I have.

Using the research of geologists who have studied this region of the Atlantic seafloor, this book shows how in the dim past of human history, the Mid-Atlantic Ridge was lifted well above sea level for long periods of time. During those sojourns above the waves, flora and fauna, as well as humans, may easily have established themselves upon the craggy landscape that was once, to coin a phrase, that antediluvian world.

My methodically based explanation isn't that hard to understand; I've tried to avoid a complicated scientific monologue. But I do believe that it creates a new and more serious debate over whether Atlantis could have ever really existed. You can be the judge, and the scientific world can weigh in with opinions, but I assure you, it won't be possible to mount an easy, slam-dunk dismissal of what you are about to read.

I'd like to make an important point concerning my qualifications to write this book. My training is not in geology; I'm from the world of materials science. I spent most of my career conducting scientific research in the subspecialty of materials evaluation, a discipline that examines the properties of materials, their strengths and weaknesses, and seeks to identify and locate the flaws that may lie inside. The materials from which the earth is composed—minerals, metals, and liquids—are the ones I have dealt with myself, both at high and low temperatures. Geologists model the slabs of crust in very much the same way that materials scientists deal with concrete and metal structural beams.

The instruments geologists use to produce images of the earth's interior—those that measure and locate the epicenters of earthquakes, as well as the ones they use to image the seafloor—all operate under the very same principles as the various instruments I employed in aerospace, nuclear power, and marine architecture. These are technologies in which I am a recognized expert. In fact, among the eighteen patents I've been awarded, many are for developing improvements to equipment that operates under the principles used by geologists. So, my investigation of Atlantis is performed with a reasonable knowledge of the tools and scientific understanding of the materials of the earth at the disposal of the geologist.

As I've become familiar with the tools of geology and basic theories, I've been able to draw conclusions that appear to lead to certain inevitabilities, such as the view that the Mid-Atlantic Ridge undergoes substantial up-and-down excursions. I'm not scoffing at the field of geology for not seeing what I believe I do, but as with any creative endeavor, someone will be the first to notice that which escapes the attention of the general community. I strongly feel this to be the case and present my findings within this context.

Finally, I'd like to add that the book is written with reference to over eighty scholarly papers, listed at the end of the book, which provide support for my theory.

That aside, I'm now prepared to take you on a fascinating adventure that provides an explanation of the things that happened to set the stage for the events that may bear directly on one of the greatest legends of Western civilization, a story with the potential to change the way we view the very history of humankind itself.

CHAPTER 1
PAST THE EVENT HORIZON OF HISTORY

In the early 1970s I worked as a cataloger in the Research Library of the American Museum of Natural History in New York, a library that few know exists, even though it happens to be one of the largest natural history libraries in the world. Through my tenure there, I had access behind the scenes and could observe the world of archaeology and ancient artifacts in ways only working in a museum could provide. In my position, I conducted research into centuries-old tomes that still contained archaic indexing identifications, such as the Paris Bookseller's classification, outdated Dewey Decimals, and so forth, and I was part of the library's program to re-catalog them according to the Library of Congress indexing nomenclature. At one time, many libraries had their own system or merely shelved books according to when they were acquired or some other arbitrary classification. The museum's library possessed thousands of volumes that were a jumble of various cataloging systems. The job of re-cataloging them was enormous.

However, because of my assignment to determine how each volume fit into the Library of Congress system, it afforded me the access to see firsthand many of the antiquities stored in the museum's fifth-floor research level.

As I sat down to write this book, those memories came back to me—the musty smells, the dry and fragile pages of ancient books, the corners of some pages unavoidably crumbling in my hands, reduced to brown, powdery fragments on my white cotton protective gloves. Many books from the late 1800s had stereo viewers and pockets on the inside cover to hold the viewers that were used for looking at daguerreotypes in 3D. Many were bound in magnificent gold-leafed bindings with extraordinary maps and strange depictions of newly discovered animals that are commonplace today.

Yet the oldest of these dusty books went back only a thousand years at most, whereas the story of Atlantis dates back over ten thousand years: thousands of years before the building of the pyramids in Egypt and Stonehenge in England, back to the time of the woolly mammoths and saber-toothed tigers and the twilight of the last ice age. When I think how much older the story of Atlantis is, it's easy to see how it might simply have dwindled down to the fragments of a foggy tale retold by a single man. How the story could have easily been completely lost to all time but, by happenstance, was not.

The details of much of what transpired ten thousand years ago remain a puzzle to which most of the pieces are missing. Our ability to interpret the fragments left by our ancestors sorely stretches the limits of our capabilities. The meaning of the artifacts in our pitiful collection comprising arrowheads, cave paintings, and marks left on animal bones continues to elude a full understanding of what they represent about the total capabilities of those who made them. The best of those versed in the field of archaeology continue to argue about the context, meaning, and importance of these meager remnants left behind by humans living many thousands of years ago. But it isn't so surprising when we consider that scholars continue to argue about events that have taken place only a few centuries ago!

So, how would we recognize a piece of Atlantis that lay buried out of context? Surprisingly, we have one. Such an out-of-context artifact resided in the National Archaeological Museum of Athens for fifty years before it was recognized for what it might have been and another twenty years before it was recognized for what it actually was: an intricate gear-driven machine. The Antikythera mechanism, as it is called, named for the island near which it was found, is an amazing bronze astronomical calculator dredged from the Aegean around the turn of the twentieth century that has been dated back to about the second or third century BCE and was at first barely recognizable as anything made by man (see figure 1). Yet despite its poor condition, enough of it has survived for it to be identified for what it is, when no other examples of this same technology have. So, how much of a civilization could we expect to survive over the course of eleven thousand years? It's doubtful that this was the only example of the technology that was made in this period. Any others that were made then must have been completely lost to us today.

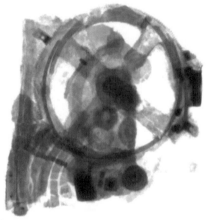

Figure 1. Top, the Antikythera mechanism as it was found in the sunken wreckage.

Middle, X-ray image that revealed the inner workings of the mechanism.

Bottom, a reconstruction of what the gear mechanism probably looked like originally.

In my short tenure at the museum, I learned to appreciate the approach taken by archaeologists and anthropologists in delving into these ancient remains of humankind.

I came to appreciate, too, the objective approach and care they took to eliminate the slant of personal points of view and bias when piecing together the meaning of the artifacts, in particular, by using the context of the setting in which they found them.

So, it is understandable that the story told by Plato is difficult to reconcile because the things archaeologists have found and know of the period in which he places his lost world seem to have no relevant context to a civilization depicted in his dialogues about Atlantis. In the spirit of this book, I am not trying to convince anyone that there was an ancient civilization where one should not be according to the beliefs of historians, anthropologists, and archaeologists. And to this end, this book is not so much about my belief in antediluvian civilizations as it is about the place it is said to have been located. In Plato's discourses on Atlantis, he touches on some interesting aspects in his description of where it was located that strongly convey to me the possibility that his references are more than coincidence if they are taken from a geologic perspective.

Plato could not have placed Atlantis in a better location as a place of confluent and titanic geologic activity. He could not have imagined a more appropriate location for his catastrophic depictions of a sunken island in the Atlantic, where today is found the Mid-Atlantic Ridge (MAR), a place of enormous volcanic capriciousness, a realm to match his imaginary apocalyptic prose. One may say that it was just a coincidence. However, the more I investigated, the more I was intrigued by the possibilities that suggested that—putting aside the aspects of a grand civilization—it might really have been just where Plato said.

What I'm suggesting is that the geologic dynamics behind the submerged MAR are just what is needed to drive some drastic prehistoric geological changes. As we see, the MAR can create vast volcanic eruptions and drive the continents apart as the engine of continental drift. So, the MAR assumes a substantial position in my theory for its power and location and for why the same forces that drove the continents caused Atlantis to rise above sea level and eventually reverse its course by sinking once again.

The mists in which Atlantis would have been shrouded have blown away into the dark recesses of time so long ago that it would have been ancient even to the architects planning the construction of the Egyptian pyramids.

I agree it is uncertain whether I could show that there ever was something we could consider a civilization once living on a large island in the Atlantic Ocean. But I believe that, at one time, such a place would have afforded a fertile, dry habitat in which plants and animals could live and thrive under the sunny skies of the mid-Atlantic. However, one thing I'm sure of is that there was once dry land on the MAR at a time in the very distant past.

CHAPTER 2
PLATO'S ATLANTIS

At its northeastern corner, the shores of the Mediterranean tumble down to the Aegean in a shamble of islands and jagged coastlines. Along this coast, the sea has ravaged ships for millennia, yet this land also has nurtured the seeds of Western civilization. Here the Greek civilization arose, building edifices and a culture and democracy that were intertwined through philosophy. These Greek philosophers—who crafted their words into the framework of cogent thought of whom and what we are as a species and what we can become—walked these rocky shores and admired these rugged works of nature.

Along the hillsides, dotted in neat profusion, the villages of man are embedded and at times cling to the slopes, standing in contrast to the angular fractals of nature. Occasionally one can find, rising in geometry completely at odds with nature in its premeditated form, the temples and structures of extraordinary design. They characterized the Greeks and all the humans who came after as those who undo the secrets of nature. For the Greeks formulated the means of logical discourse, chipping and hammering at physical, philosophical, and metaphysical questions until they yielded answers. Or, if not, they provided the tools for the generations that followed to attack the problems until they collapsed in exhaustion into a heap of disciplined thought and knowledge.

Among the keenest of minds of the ancient world, one man stood above these giants of contemplation, a student of Socrates and the mentor of Aristotle. Revered by his contemporaries and studied by the generations to follow, Plato (c. 320 BCE) spoke in weighted words that carried the essence of human imagination. Plato set the standard for the logical treatment of the questions with which man is inevitably faced. He debated the issues of who we are, what we are, and what we should do with our extraordinary ability to shape ourselves as well as the world around us.

But at odds with all his other works, which are required reading in literature and philosophy classes today, Plato makes an assertion that has created nothing but controversy. He claimed in two connected dialogues that a civilization comparable to that of classical Greece once inhabited a large island called Atlantis lying off the coast of what is today Spain and Portugal. Plato also claimed that as far back as nine thousand years before his time (more than eleven thousand years before the present), this civilization, which, according to him, flourished for centuries, was destroyed. He depicted it as sinking and quickly falling into the dark recesses of history to be all but forgotten. If not for Plato's account, described in *Critias* and *Timaeus*, Atlantis may never have been a topic for the present world to debate, the search for it never taken up. There are no known accounts of Atlantis contemporary to Plato; any mentions thereafter must be attributed to what Plato wrote first.

According to Plato, in referring to this island kingdom as Atlantis, he did not choose a name of his own derivation but came by it as part of an elaborate legend passed down to him through his family. Plato reminisced that he was ten years old when he heard the story of Atlantis, told by Critias the younger, who was at that time in his nineties. Critias spoke during a festival, probably Apaturia, and said how his great-grandfather was told by Dropides, another Plato relative, of a story told to him by Solon. Solon was a well-respected statesman and reputable historical source during his lifetime.

Solon was a figure renowned to historians today. He was well traveled and in his journeys, according to Plato, spent some time in Egypt. Plato wrote through Critias's voice that while in Egypt, Solon was the guest of the priests who watched over the sacred tombs and monuments in the city of Sais. The priests told Solon of what they believed to be a historical account of the kingdom and island fortress that once lay in the Atlantic Ocean.

In Plato's description, the large island existed beyond the Pillars of Heracles, at the western end of the Mediterranean Sea. Today, we know the Pillars of Heracles, which still present an imposing landform, as the Strait of Gibraltar. I've been unable to find any Egyptian record to corroborate what Plato claims Solon learned. Although this doesn't mean the claim isn't true, I can't otherwise offer any strong support.

I never intended to provide a lengthy dissertation on Plato and his dialogues except for the sake of understanding from where the legend arose and the context in which it was presented. However, I think it's worth presenting a cursory recital of the original tale. Therein are the clues that provide the compelling motivation to disambiguate his embellishments from what seem to be historical accounts. I use the word "embellishments" because all I can say about the Atlantean island concerns the geological aspects. The fact that Plato provides these descriptions of elaborate palaces and cities is something that I have no way of corroborating. They make interesting images but add nothing to determining whether the island ever existed.

He was clearly aware of a legend that was based on the fact that there was at one time a large, populated island in the Atlantic. The mystery of such a place may easily have been enough to stir the imagination of those over eleven millennia ago to carry the myth forward to the times of the Egyptians and in turn find its way through a family member to Plato. These claims are difficult to substantiate. But in contrast, the clues concerning the location of the island of Atlantis is something that can be investigated.

As Robert Payne notes in his book The Gold of Troy, Heinrich Schliemann discovered the ancient city of Homer's epics, confirming that it was indeed a real place. But Schliemann had to fight an uphill battle in his search for Troy because the commonly held belief at the time was to the contrary, that Homer's depiction of Troy was fictitious. However, though Troy turned out to be a real place in history, it was also patently obvious that the Olympian gods were not participating in a soap opera–like existence with real men. Consequently, proving the existence of Troy didn't make Zeus any more of a real entity. As for Plato, his descriptions of the god Poseidon and the demigod Atlas in the *Timaeus* and *Critias* could be compared to Homer's depictions of the Olympians. It doesn't make what Plato says about the island of Atlantis any less real; it just speaks to the context from which historical events have been written, with an obliging acknowledgment to those supernatural beings.

Of course, there are a multitude of authors who have written about Atlantis as a real place in history. But those taking Plato's side could not find a way to tangibly show that he was, in fact, a historian. On the other hand, the preponderance of the academic world considers Atlantis a wholly fabricated story by Plato, used to drive a philosophical point about an ideal political state.

I'm not alone in the academic world in believing that Plato was truly a historian, for the well-respected scholar and author Mary Settegast is of the same opinion.

In her book *Plato, Prehistorian* (1990), Settegast makes a convincing case that Plato was reciting historical events in the *Critias* and *Timaeus*. In the *Critias*, Plato describes the conversations and discussions that take place in the course of what was the holiday festival of Apaturia. Plato describes how the characters of the dialogue are obliged to retell stories handed down from generation to generation.

Settegast points to two clues that are depicted in the way that Plato wrote the dialogues in which he reveals Atlantis. First, she believes that classical Greek values would have prohibited Plato from using a pious holiday as the setting for his characters. Second, she points to the stature of the characters who carry out the discourse throughout the preponderance of the dialogue. The speakers are all Greek citizens who were held in high esteem by the Athenians, and it would have been insulting to depict them as coconspirators in a fabricated tale.

For someone living in a time when there was no apparent common understanding of what lay west of the Mediterranean Sea, Plato demonstrated an amazing ability to depict an accurate account of unknown geography. For instance, he insisted that the island civilization of Atlantis was situated beyond the Gates of Heracles. This is where the sunken outline of the MAR can now be found. Today it is submerged, but in a time nine thousand years before Plato, it appears that it may have been above sea level.

According to my hypothesis, the ending of the last ice age triggered the sinking of Atlantis. But the last ice age was just one of many. Prior to the last ice age, there was an interglacial period where the climate was warm enough to melt the previous glaciers. It is also true that there were several interglacial periods, according to geologists, and many instances when the island of Atlantis could have risen, only to sink again.

Plato depicted Atlantis's beginnings as a smaller island consisting of some slight hills that rose higher above sea level with time. As it ascended, those hills might very well have evolved into mountains.

The island that would be Atlantis, which I believe was the MAR, is still a place of constant volcanic eruptions powerful enough to move the continents apart. This turns out to be a very believable location for the island if one can show how it gets from six thousand feet below sea level to over a thousand feet above sea level.

The time of the Atlantis myth, as told by Plato, occurred during a geologic period of great change. The ice age [that fostered enormous glaciers that covered the continents] were beginning to melt at the same time that Plato claimed Atlantis began to sink.

Through this next aspect of his references to Atlantis, Plato, once again through Critias, tries to assure his listeners, who are gathered for a major religious holiday, that the story he was about to tell—and even as he tells it—is not a fabrication. Plato was obviously going out of his way to stress the fact that this was a true story, not the kind of allegorical story he might have used as a tool to enhance one of his opinions or lessons. As you can see from the following quotes, he makes this point twice at the outset, once through Critias and then again through Socrates:

> Critias: *"Then listen, Socrates, to a tale which, though strange, is certainly true, having been attested by Solon, who was the wisest of the seven sages."*

> Socrates: *"Very good. And what is this ancient famous action of the Athenians, which Critias declared, on the authority of Solon, to be not a mere legend, but an actual fact?"*

So, if Plato was truly writing an allegory, he might not have gone so far out of his way to emphatically insist that it was without question a true accounting of history. It is impossible to know for certain whether he was writing an allegory or a history, and for this alone there is no clear-cut answer to what Plato meant to convey. The fact that it leaves room for interpretation is, in and of itself, a cause to assume what we want.

In yet another example of Plato's attempt to create the atmosphere of a factual account rather than an allegorical tale to make a point, he discussed the fact that the characters of the dialogue have Greek as opposed to foreign names. He goes very much out of his way to make this point by having Critias say:

> *"Yet, before proceeding further in the narrative, I ought to warn you, that you must not be surprised if you should perhaps hear Hellenic names given to foreigners. I will tell you the reason of this: Solon, who was intending to use the tale for his poem, enquired into the meaning of the names, and found that the early Egyptians in writing them down had translated them into their own language, and he recovered the meaning of the several*

names and when copying them out again translated them into our language. My great-grandfather, Dropides, had the original writing, which is still in my possession, and was carefully studied by me when I was a child. Therefore, if you hear names such as are used in this country, you must not be surprised, for I have told how they came to be introduced."

This is a rather long-winded explanation for something that needn't have been brought up to begin with unless you wanted to clearly convey the sense that it was a real account of historical events. I realize that one could think otherwise, but his continual persistence that this was a historical account forces me to further consider his sincerity.

But the question of truth or fairy tale aside, we should continue to examine the fascinating elements Plato drops into his story. Within Plato's recounting of the story of Atlantis, he mentions a very interesting fact that should have led to more discussion from those seeking to resolve the question of what veracity we may attribute to his story of Atlantis. Plato discusses not only the large island, which he claims to be larger than Libya and Asia (or did he mean Asia Minor?) together, but also goes on to say that the Atlantic Ocean was navigable before the sinking. He further insinuates that it was not navigable after the sinking.

Plato states that beyond Atlantis, one would find yet another continent, a landmass apparently not known to the people of Plato's time. That continent could only be interpreted as North America—surely a place one would encounter, sailing past an elevated Mid-Atlantic Ridge. North America was certainly considered an almost boundless continent to its first settlers, and it does surround a large portion of the North Atlantic. If considering North and South America as one continent, the two clearly dwarfed what we now know as Europe.

I find it uncanny that within the context of a supposed fable, Plato recounted geography that was not commonly known until the Vikings crossed the vast reaches of the Atlantic and discovered North America over a thousand years later and that wouldn't become commonly known across Europe until fifteen hundred years on. Furthermore, Plato seemed aware that the Mediterranean is much smaller than the Atlantic. That's another fact that wasn't known to the mapmakers of Plato's time and wouldn't be known to the world until long after that. Of course, there is the chance that these things are a coincidence, but it would have been an amazingly prophetic guess.

There's also the issue of where Plato placed the alleged Atlantean island in his tale and its correspondence to the size, situation, and shape of the MAR. According to Plato, Atlantis was situated in the Atlantic Ocean, off the coast of Spain. This is exactly where one finds the MAR. So, in that regard, Plato looks prescient for his time. He somehow is able to pinpoint a large landmass that could satisfy his claim for the location of a substantial sunken island.

As to the size of the island that was once above the waves, Plato claimed it to be as big as Libya and Asia combined. However, if we examine the bulge in the MAR where you would also find the Azores Plateau, it would seem that the sea level could never be low enough for an island to form that was as sizeable as he claimed—that is, as large as we all agree Asia to be today. In order to account for this discrepancy, we should consider Plato's understanding of the extent of Asia. His perspective can easily be understood if one realizes that at one time the Greeks considered present-day Turkey, which they knew as Anatolia, to be the extent of Asia. It also could have been an ambiguous reference to the Persian Empire, which included Turkey and also Libya. When writing these dialogues, Plato clearly didn't think that, two thousand years later, people would still be reading them or that, by then, the idea of what was considered Asia would be quite different. The map in figure 2 provides a graphic representation of what Plato might have conceived of as Asia.

Figure 2. The Persian Empire in the Achaemenid era, sixth century BC.

From Cyrene, in Libya, to Baghdad is about sixteen hundred miles, which is in the extent that I predict the MAR might rise above sea level under the right conditions.

If Plato was describing the size of Atlantis from the point of view of the way it looked as one approached it from the sea rather than from that of a two-dimensional map, then it might have taken on a whole different appearance. Allow me to explain.

The way that the MAR is situated in the Atlantic, it appears to run along a line from north to south. When the MAR was raised above sea level, it would have been only a few hundred miles in width, east to west. Its length, north to south, would have been approximately fifteen hundred miles long, according to my most conservative estimates. So, sailing out from Spain toward Atlantis, one would have come upon a landmass of great extent that appeared to have an endless shoreline. Anyone sailing its entire length either north or south would have had this conclusion reinforced as they found approximately fifteen hundred miles of coastline. But the length of the main island and the thousands of smaller ones along its shores would have disguised the extent of its width; the lasting impression of Atlantis would certainly have been one of enormity.

Plato went on to elaborate on the civilization, discussing the details of the kings who ruled, the structure of the buildings, and how the center of Atlantis was constructed in the form of several concentric rings, like circular canals. Whether any of these claims are true is beyond consideration for the moment, because there is no way to verify any of it unless the ruins were to be discovered.

CHAPTER 3
THE MYSTERY OF THE MOVING CONTINENTS

I live on a large, narrow island just outside New York City called—no, not Atlantis—but, quite appropriately, Long Island. The American Indians named it Paumanok, land of tribute, but in renaming it, the European settlers, judging its shape, were more practical. It's only about a sixty-mile drive from where I live to the tip of Long Island, where I can look out onto the vast expanse of the Atlantic Ocean.

The tip of Long Island, Montauk Point, is a popular vacation spot known for its beaches and fishing and for the big ocean waves that bully the shore, attracting scores of surfers. This sandy island was formed during what was known as the Wisconsin Glaciations, some twenty-one thousand years ago. As the waning glaciers of that last ice age slowed their progress to a halt, they left a leading edge of debris, called moraines, and in the southern part of New York State, they piled up into this long, fish-shaped island that is now a major suburb of New York City. There've been several periods of glaciations in the past, and this one drove great walls of ice like mighty plows against the landscape, forming all manner of interesting landforms and leaving enormous out-of-place boulders, called erratics, scattered across the landscape.

Scientists of the early nineteenth century had no idea what process had formed the odd V-shaped valleys, the moraines, and the erratics that they observed around the Northern Hemisphere because they weren't aware that there had previously been dramatic climatological changes that would someday become known as the ice ages. In 1840, Louis Agassiz published the founding work on ice ages, Étude *sur les Glaciers*, which presented his theory that there had been, at one time in the recent geological past, a period of glaciations in which the temperate zones of much of the earth were covered with enormous glaciers. The Wisconsin Glaciations were the last of these alternating, expanding, and receding glacial packs that included very short periods of warming in between.

These epochs, when the great ice packs crept outward from the poles to cover the adjacent landmasses, caused the oceans to lose vast quantities of water. The ocean levels dropped greatly from what they are today, and it is difficult to understand what that meant to the planet. The oceans are so vast that it's hard to imagine how much ice would have had to form into glaciers to lower the oceans hundreds of feet. But the earth is constantly in flux; furthermore, the oceans themselves are forever changing size and shape as a result of the drifting continents.

Standing on the windswept, rocky breakwater at Montauk Point, the farthermost point in New York State before one leaves North America altogether, before the seemingly endless expanse of the Atlantic begins, it is almost inconceivable that this immense ocean at one time did not exist. But it is true—the Atlantic Ocean has not always been one of the earth's great surface features. Once, around 225 million years ago, North America was solidly connected to Africa. In fact, back then, I would have been able to step off one of the rocks on which I'm standing and walk forward right into western Africa, to an area that is, today, just south of Morocco and the Atlas Mountains.

Of course, I can't do that because there it is, the Atlantic Ocean, the second largest body of water on the planet. The earth is 4.5 billion years old, though this immense watery expanse has been around for just a fraction of that time. What caused Africa and North America to separate? Or, more broadly and more puzzling still, *how* could they have separated, and so rapidly? How could these huge sections of the earth's crust have been ripped apart and sent on a journey of over three thousand miles in such a short time, geologically speaking?

After only about forty million years, when the formation of the Atlantic was well underway, I'd no longer be looking at Africa, because it would have drifted six hundred miles east. That seems like a lot even after forty million years, so I have to do the math. Wait, don't turn the page—it's a very simple calculation.

First, we need to know how quickly the continents are separating on their drifting path. To do that, geologists have come up with an ingenious method of counting lines of magnetism in the rocks. Just as tree rings enable us to tell how old a tree is, these magnetic lines do the same for large slabs of rock. A century ago, geologists noticed that some volcanic rock contained magnetic stripes. It turns out that the stripes have alternating polarity. So, if one puts a magnet near a stripe, it reveals if it's a north or south pole by whether the magnet is attracted or repelled. It was discovered that one set of the stripes is the same polarity as the current magnetic field the earth possesses. Consequently, the alternate stripe is opposite of the earth's magnetic field—the magnetic field that allows a compass to point north. But disturbingly, it meant that at one time the earth's magnetic field was pointing in the opposite direction.

The reason that the rocks had these alternating magnetic fields was also a mystery until it was realized that it was an aspect of the cooling of the magma from which the rock was made.

It wasn't until the late 1960s when the Vine-Matthews-Morley hypothesis proposed that oceanic volcanism, which caused the continents to move, showed a striped pattern of reversals of the earth's magnetic field in the cooled volcanic rock and could be used as a measure of the rate at which continents moved. When the magma erupts from a spreading center, it has no magnetic field until it cools. As it hardens, it gets magnetized with the direction of the earth's magnetic field at that moment in time. Over the last twenty million years, the earth's magnetic field has reversed about every two hundred thousand to three hundred thousand years. It hasn't done this lately, however, for over seven hundred thousand years. So, it's due for another reversal any time now.

The rate at which the continents are sliding apart turned out to be, on average, two centimeters per year. There are some spreading centers where that rate is faster or slower than others.

Now back to our calculation. If the continents are separating by about two centimeters, or a little less than an inch, a year—I'm rounding everything off as we go—we next need to know how many inches equal a mile. We start with the number of feet in a mile:

5,280 feet = 1 mile

Next, we need to change feet to inches to calculate how many inches are in a mile:

12 inches × 5,280 = 63,360 inches to a mile

So, if the continents move an inch a year, after forty million years, the continents will have moved forty million inches. How many miles is that?

40,000,000 inches/63,600 inches per mile = 631 miles

The same holds true for the way the Atlantic formed over hundreds of millions of years, separating North America from Africa and Europe by thousands of miles. Even though it's a painfully slow process, the continents can move thousands of miles over millions of years.

Going back to what I was saying about how the Atlantic formed originally, Africa and North America were joined as part of a precursor continent known to geologists as Pangaea. As we now know, before the opening of the Atlantic, North America and Africa were joined together, but if one waits long enough, one will find all the continents very far apart.

So then, after waiting a mere forty million years, I would now have to travel to Africa from North America in a ship, on a voyage of a couple of days instead of one step forward from the rock on which I'm standing. Today the distance of open water is quite a bit farther, and so is Africa.

Because Africa and North America are now thousands of miles apart, it's obvious that some extraordinary force must be at play that continues to push these staggeringly large landmasses great distances away from each other. These geological processes operate on time scales measured in millions and billions of years, whereas the lifetime of plants and animals are measured in a minuscule fraction of that. The flora and fauna carried along by the drifting continents have time to undergo dramatic evolutionary changes. Some plants and animals living on the drifting continents have encountered a great degree of genetic divergence, disguising, though not erasing, their original genetic heritage. Some plants and animals have retained enough of their outward appearance that it is noticeable. On opposite shores of separated continents, we find animals and plants that are different. Monkeys living in South America have prehensile tails, and the ones living in Africa do not. But being so far apart, one would not suspect that they originated from the same precursor monkey that once lived when the continents were originally joined. The same could be said for the origins of plants. The fauna and flora did not betray the fact that the continents were joined.

But the fossils of plants and animals that were embedded in the rocks couldn't change in form at all. Scientists in the past began to find that one side of the ocean had the identical fossil fauna and flora as the other. And so, the diverging continents left behind clues about how they were once connected, by the discovery of the fossils of the flora and fauna left behind on opposite coastlines.

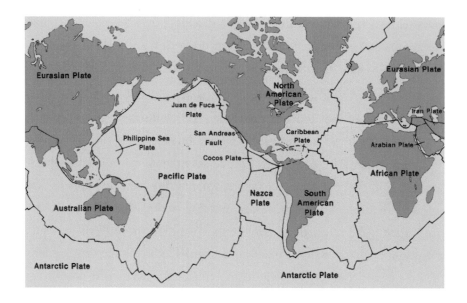

Figure 3. *Plates that make up the crust of the earth that carry the continents with them as they move relative to each other.*

The obvious similarities of life-forms on opposite continents presented a conundrum for these early eighteenth- and nineteenth-century scientists; they saw the similarities among organisms on different continents but couldn't understand how they had become separated by such great distances of open waters. Later, the similarities of rock formations themselves on opposite continents added to the frustration.

The geologic forces and processes that drive the continents apart are the basis of the study of plate tectonics: the theory that has revealed an earth divided into a series of massive slabs of its crust, called plates (see figure 3). These plates are floating on far hotter strata of rock below it, the asthenosphere. This layer of the mantle is spongy enough to allow magma rising up in plumes of colossal convection currents to punch through the earth's crust and provide the enormous power needed to move around the continental plates from one location on the surface to another. Magma is the superheated rock passing through the asthenosphere from deep inside the earth. Lava, on the other hand, is what we call magma that has poured out onto the surface. A parsed difference, sort of like that between meteors and meteorites, the latter being what actually hits the ground. The lava is what cools to form the rock and is magnetized by the earth's magnetic field. It is the action of the lava oozing out of the spreading centers that pushes the continents apart.

Abraham Ortelius, credited with developing the first modern atlas, *Thesaurus Geographicus*, proposed continental drift in the mid- to late 1500s to explain why South America and Africa appear to fit together so well. To provide a rationale for how the continents were able to move, he postulated that earthquakes had torn the continents apart and that floods had filled in the space in between. Figure 4 is a map by Antonio Snider-Pellegrini, an early depiction of how continental drift worked on a qualitative level.

Figure 4. *Antonio Snider-Pellegrini created this map in 1858, depicting the continents of South America and Africa before and after they separated, according to his theory of why the landmasses have such closely matching coastlines.*

This concept of mobile continents was originally referred to as continental drift (in German, *Kontinentalverschiebung*: the translation, literally, "continental moving"), in a theory formulated in 1912 by Alfred Wegener, a German climatologist (see figure 5).

Wegener's theory was greeted quite coolly by the scientific community, partly because he was delving into a field that wasn't his expertise (kind of like me); after all, he was a climatologist—a weatherman to the established world of geology.

Furthermore, his theory employed nothing more than inference to justify his argument. It was a theory that explained many aspects of the problem that had faced geologists and mapmakers ever since the coastlines of Africa and South America were accurately drawn. The question remained: How did the coastlines come to look so similar if at one time they weren't joined together? And if they were once joined together, how did they become so widely separated? Along came Wegener with a theory that explained the obvious fit of these coastlines and other related issues, as well as the match of flora, fauna, and rock formations, but he could not mount a geophysical explanation to account for this continental excursion theory. Nobody was buying Wegener's theory without some geophysics behind it.

When pushed to explain how the continents could have moved, Wegener speculated that one of two, or both, of the rotational forces might be the source of the drift mechanism. He offered the theory that the earth's spin, causing centrifugal forces on the landmasses, might have spun them enough to crack the crust and send it drifting. He further speculated that the precession of the earth's axis could also be a motivator. As a side suggestion, he noted that the mid-ocean ridges are constantly cracking and pouring magma to the surface, and in that may lie some evidence. As close as he was to explaining the actual mechanism of continental drift with the volatile oceanic ridge proposal, he mentioned it only in passing and never brought it up in later writings or discussions.

During Wegener's entire lifetime, the notion that the continents could move was far too difficult to comprehend and so it was rejected out of hand by the mainstream scientific community. Within the context of the understanding of geology in the early 1900s, it's not hard to understand how the scientific community might have had a hard time with this concept; it is still difficult for many today to wrap their heads around it.

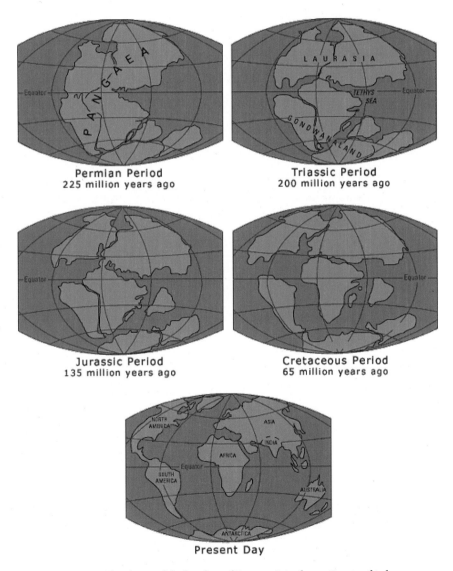

Figure 5. *The phases of the breakup of Pangaea into the continents of today.*

Wegener was faced with the same puzzle that nineteenth-century geologists struggled with and is one every grade-school child may notice the first time a teacher displays a map of the world for the class. The continents of South America and Africa appear to fit together in a perfect jigsaw puzzle match. Undaunted, throughout his life Wegener continued to pursue evidence in support of his theory. He noted that plant and animal fossils, as well as geologic structures on both continents, quite remarkably matched up, and he collected data that he hoped would eventually support his theory. But the conclusive data came too late for Wegener. He never got to experience the satisfaction of knowing he was right. Unfortunately, he froze to death while trekking across Greenland in 1930, three decades before the conclusive supporting evidence was discovered in the late 1960s.

So, during Wegener's lifetime, the question for geologists remained: Why did these matching coastlines, flora and fauna, and geologic formations make it appear that the continents were once connected to each other? There were too many similarities for it to be coincidence but not enough of a geological foundation to explain what had happened.

Certainly, South America couldn't have cracked off Africa and somehow drifted away to its present position thousands of miles west. If that were the case, where would the South Atlantic basin have come from to fill the space in between? What force could be powerful enough to actually move a continent? Where would the crust of the earth go that once occupied the space into which South America now found itself? Or had the ocean bottom stretched elastically all the way across the Atlantic?

Ortelius had had the same problem explaining his primitive theory back in the 1500s, and he opted to describe it in the only way that scientists of his day understood geologic activity, which was by an earthquake and flood methodology. But no one could explain how earthquakes could cause the continents to separate on such grand scales.

In the late nineteenth century, Roberto Mantovani, an Italian geologist and musician, offered another fascinating, if bizarre, approach to making sense of the intriguing matches of coastlines, flora, fauna, and rock formations. He had visited Reunion Island, in the Indian Ocean, in 1878, staying long enough to witness the volcanic activity creating huge fractures along the flanks of the volcano that formed the shoreline. He extrapolated that observation to a worldview of the fracturing of the continents driven by the expansion of the earth's crust. His theory evolved to include a hypothesis that the earth was expanding like a balloon, as it once was covered in the original crust that stretched to the point of fracturing to form the continents as they now appeared, very much as he had seen along the slopes of the volcano on Reunion Island.

There hasn't been a dearth of theories to explain how the continents could have drifted apart. Another theory, proposed by William Henry Pickering, who also predicted the existence of Pluto, speculated that the moon was once part of the earth. Because of some imbalance in the earth's mass, the moon had ripped away from the earth at the Pacific Ocean basin, leaving the seabed as a scar but, more importantly, also causing a then-existing single continent's crust to break up and drift apart. I remember being taught a similar theory in grade school in the early 1950s. But all these theories had issues that were unexplainable. When did the earth stop expanding, because it no longer was? How had the moon torn away from the earth, and why hadn't it done more damage than leave a scar and serenely drifting continents? There were other theories with other geological issues, none of which were acceptable to the scientific community.

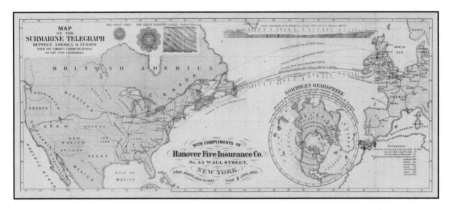

Figure 6. Nineteenth-century map of the telegraph cable-laying route that first alerted the scientific community of the existence of the MAR.

But despite the apparent absurdity that the continents could move, there remained the compelling questions of matching coastlines, fossils, and life-forms that could not be answered by any other explanation. As close as Wegener was, even his theory fell short of an explanation the geological community could embrace.

Up until the late 1950s and early 1960s, the world of science was still clueless, although there were hints to the puzzle that had gone unrecognized. In 1872, a team of scientists aboard the HMS *Challenger*, which was charting the seafloor in preparation for laying transoceanic telegraph cable, discovered a submerged mountain range midway across the Atlantic Ocean (see figure 6). In subsequent cable-laying operations, there were occasions when the cables had to be pulled back up or adjusted with grappling hooks. On occasion, the hooks snagged chunks of volcanic rock as they struggled with the cable. The mountain range and volcanic rock were the first of two clues that would eventually help to unravel the mystery of the drifting continents.

But the technology and scale to properly collect and analyze the essential data that was required to explain this mystery were yet to be invented. Even geologists of the early twentieth century, who had come to an understanding of relativity and quantum mechanics, couldn't crack the mystery of the drifting continents. They would be amazed at how morphologically different the seafloor was from the continental crust than they had ever imagined.

But the time was nearing when the clues, the technology, and the understanding of geophysics would be in place to create the biggest revelation in the world of geology.

CHAPTER 4
THE ENIGMA OF THE SUNKEN MOUNTAIN

Only in the last fifty years have geologists come to realize that the sea-floors are very different from the continental landmasses. The seafloors comprise most of the earth's crust yet are very inaccessible, and only until recently have they been shown to have quite distinct origins and structures than were earlier believed. Up until the mid-1960s, the ocean floors were thought to be merely a series of basins in the earth's crust, largely the same in origin as the continents, though it was not known how each ended up with such different geologic formation and structure. This simplistic view was the understanding held from the earliest times of modern geology, going back to the seventeenth century.

Comprehensive physical evidence returned from the explorations of the National Science Foundation–sponsored Deep Sea Drilling Project [from 1968 to 1983] revealed revolutionary discoveries about the structure of the earth's crust, especially concerning the areas lying under the sea.

Their first basic discovery, and now the foundation of modern geology, was that the crust of the earth floats on the less dense and somewhat molten rock beneath it (see figure 7). The second discovery was that these buoyant continents were not only afloat but also moving relative to each other, at places diverging, at others converging. The third discovery was that all along the ocean floors were mid-ocean mountain ranges behaving as spreading centers, which provided the mechanism that propelled the continents along their drifting paths. And finally there was the equally startling discovery that at points of plate convergence, one plate slides under another, creating subduction zones that remelt continental and ocean crust.

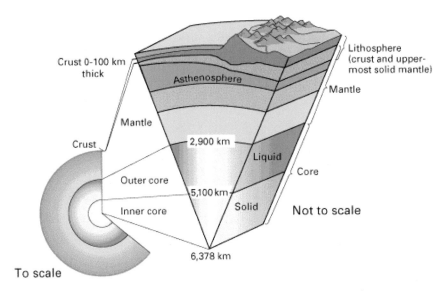

Figure 7. The layers of the earth's crust, mantle, and core in this US Geological Survey diagram.

These discoveries formed the focus of the new field of geologic investigation known today as plate tectonics. This theory suggests that the crust of the earth is a jigsaw of slabs called plates and that the plates drift around relative to one another, leading to the term we've already discussed, continental drift. Furthermore, a still poorly understood form of convection process in the mantle is the phenomenon that drives the plates apart by effusing magma through long cracks at these spreading centers, typically at the mid-ocean ridges. The present theory of how mid-ocean ridgelines are initiated is through the action of enormous plumes of magma rising beneath the continental crust, which create cracks that split the continents apart. These magma plumes are thought to be part of cell margins that are associated with gigantic convection currents (see figure 8). These convection currents are the same as we see when we heat thick liquids, such as oils or puddings. The liquid forms regular-shaped patterns at first, and then the upwelling of the heated liquid below creates the boiling stage. In the case of the magma in the earth, the edges or margins of the regular-shaped patterns become the place where the boiling to the surface breaks through.

The continual rising and driving action along the convection current margins split apart a primordial, conjoined slab of crust that was once South America and Africa. The forces were so immense that they eventually drove those slabs apart to become separate continents. The South Atlantic ridge (the southern portion of the MAR below the Romanche Trench) is the remnant of that original departure and grows continually. India was at one time a part of Africa but was split off by an upwelling convection cell that drove the Indian subcontinent across the planet, forming the Indian Ocean basin and bringing India to where it is now. Its journey is not yet over, as it continues to collide with the Asian landmass. The Himalaya mountain range is the result of that collision; as the Indian subcontinent drove into Asia, it thrust the mountain range up the same way that pushing on a rug can create folds.

The Arabian Peninsula was thus split off from Africa and along the way created the Red Sea. Today, along the Olduvai Gorge on the interior of the African continent, a convection cell is presently at work cleaving the major portion of the continent asunder once again. Interestingly, Olduvai is where some of the earliest specimens of prehumans were found at about the same time scientists were discovering that the continents drift apart.

It is suspected that the convection cells rising from the intensely heated core of the earth consisting of hundreds of cubic miles of magma can hew the crustal rock by applying an enormous blowtorch-like heat source that weakens and finally fractures the crust.

So, it seems that the MAR is located at one of these spreading centers and, moreover, that the spreading center is what created the ridge to begin with. The height of a mid-ocean ridge at any given spreading center is dependent on the volume and rate of magma rising from below. The MAR in the North Atlantic Ocean happens to be located above the unusual confluence of three plate boundaries, as well as one of the most active hot spots, making it a particularly active region.

A hot spot in the earth's crust is a point over which a continual plume of magma flows up, at times varying over a period of millions of years. This contrasts with spreading centers, which are at the edges of convection cells and rise along one edge and fall around the opposite edges. The magma flows out onto the surface of oceanic crust along the separations of continental plates, another process that goes on for millions of years.

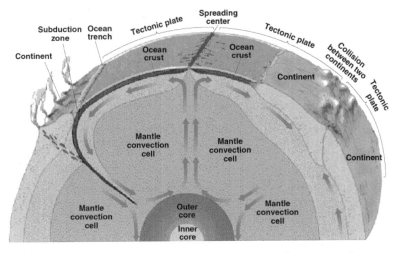

Figure 8. Schematic of convection cells that drive the continental movement and plumes that create oceanic islands.

The MAR is the highest and most geologically active of the forty thousand miles of oceanic ridges that girdle the earth, somewhat like the seams of a baseball. The MAR rises as much as seventy-seven hundred feet at some points above the seafloor. Since its discovery over one hundred years ago, it has been the object of geological interest due to its unexpected location and its surprisingly unrelenting volcanic activity.

Several scientific expeditions to the MAR have been made over the last fifty years. Some have used submersibles, deep-diving subs, to explore the depths and examine the seafloor firsthand (see figure 9). Early expeditions essentially were limited to gathering data from only the surface of the seafloor. Despite the limits of the early investigations, much valuable geological data was acquired, including the revelation that seawater infiltrates the cracked seafloor and percolates back out after coming in contact with the deeply placed, high-temperature rock strata. As the magma rises beneath the ridges, more magma arrives at the spreading centers than can be released through effusion, and a balloon effect occurs, which stretches the oceanic crust. It's what happens when a painted balloon is inflated— the dry paint cracks as the rubber expands. In doing so, the seafloor crust eventually reaches its strain limit and fractures occur. These fractures are evident throughout most of the mid-ocean ridges, and it is here that the seawater gains entry.

Figure 9. *The Alvin, an early manned deep-sea submersible.*

As the exploratory technology has evolved, another type of study technique has become an important tool in oceanic investigation. This technology is in the form of remotely controlled, sensor-arrayed equipment, such as SeaBeam, which is a side-looking sonar scanner (see figure 10). As the name implies, a sonar beam is directed sideways to the line in which the robot travels, just as a passenger in a car might look out a side window at the passing scenery.

These exploratory sonar instruments employ ultrasound, a form of sound waves that can be aimed at and bounce off formations on the sea-floor. The returning signals, which are principally reflections, are collected and converted to images—very much as dolphins and bats can do.

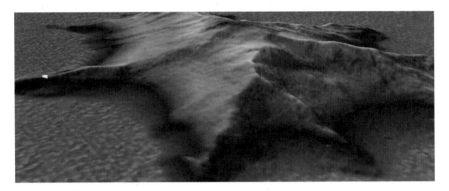

Figure 10. SeaBeam sonar mapping data.

Submersible robots have enabled specific areas of the surface of the seafloor to be mapped in three-dimensional detail. They are deployed from specially equipped ships—the one in figure 11 appropriately named *Atlantis*. The contours of the seafloor can reveal much about what geologic activity has and is transpiring below. Oil companies use these techniques in searching for petroleum deposits, and the process has been extremely useful—and, as we can imagine, it wouldn't be used by profit-minded companies if it didn't return meaningful data.

Figure 11. *The deep-sea submersible tender, aptly named Atlantis, used to deploy the submersible Alvin to extreme depths of the ocean for scientific research.*

A more challenging exploratory venture is to drill into the seafloor surface and remove core samples. The enormous difficulty here is that it is extremely demanding to maintain the ship in the same place over the drilling site. Not being able to do so will cause the long drill assembly to flop around like a wet noodle, eventually causing it to come apart. In drilling into the ocean bottom, typical water depths of over ten thousand feet must be traversed first. Only then can the drill begin to bite into the seafloor rock of the ocean basin. This technique has been perfected by the oil industry, and it accounts for much of the exploited petroleum deposits today. But the petroleum isn't found in the igneous rock created by the constant magma outpourings. The petroleum geologists are most interested in the sedimentary rock that was built up over time by the slow settling of dead sea creatures and plants during the course of millions of years. These sediments hold the organic remains of those dead creatures and plants that once inhabited the oceans above and have now transformed their organic skeletons into oil deposits.

The National Science Foundation (NSF) sponsored one of the first excursions to the ridge in 1968, the Deep Sea Drilling Project. On Leg 2, the drilling ship *Glomar Challenger* sailed from Hoboken, New Jersey, to Dakar, Senegal, in West Africa. During the crossing, it made five stops to take core samplings from the seafloor.

The *Glomar Challenger* was specially designed to meet the rigors of deep-sea drilling, with computer-controlled auxiliary propellers tied into an inertial navigation system to maintain lateral stability. They gave the ship the uncanny ability to remain virtually motionless above a fixed point on the seafloor, even in relatively high seas (see figure 12).

Figure 12. *The deep-sea drilling ship Glomar Challenger.*

This ability is essential for drilling for any length of time in deep water; without it, little would be known of the structure of the ocean crust.

The first leg of the North Atlantic voyage included thirteen different drill sites. Samples taken at sites made in depths up to15,406 feet. They immediately revealed interesting findings that suggest that the dynamics of the MAR may be somewhat more complex than was understood before.

Far overshadowed, and in a certain context perhaps rightly so, were some other discoveries that bear on the hypothesis of this book.

As an aside, it might be of interest to some to learn where the sophisticated technology of the *Glomar Challenger* was developed. This is a tale of intrigue, beginning early in 1968 with the tragic sinking of a Russian submarine fifteen hundred miles northwest of Hawaii in waters that were sixteen thousand feet deep. The US Navy sought an American industrial partner to develop a ship that could locate and raise the submarine to the surface. To assure the secrecy of the project, a cover story was developed. For this clandestine operation the partner chosen was the Hughes Corporation, which was contracted to oversee the project. Hughes created a cover story that the ship it was building was part of a plan to mine the seafloor for manganese nodules. Manganese has important uses for industrial applications, such as an alloying element in stainless steel and a corrosion-resisting alloy in aluminum soft drink and beer cans. The deep-sea recovery operation went forward without public speculation about another purpose other than the cover story released by Hughes. In fact, the cover story was so successfully distracting to the actual purpose that other companies began to investigate this manganese mining process.

The *Glomar Challenger* was able to secretly lift part of the Russian submarine to the surface and acquire some important espionage information. It was only partially successful, however, because an important part of the submarine broke off as it was being lifted and was never recovered. Subsequently, the petroleum industry community was able to transfer this technology to deep-sea drilling and locating oil deposits. Finally, the scientific community was able to use the technology for the retrieval of core samples from the deepest depths of the ocean bottom. The scientific data recovered eventually revealed intriguing facts about the nature of the MAR that went unnoticed by those interested in the search for Atlantis until now.

CHAPTER 5
CLUES TO A PUZZLE

The reason I spent so much time researching the myth of Atlantis lies in the many interesting clues that seem to present a picture of a real place and a real set of events. The case for Atlantis may not seem plausible at first, but the clues to which I refer and will enumerate going forward create a realistic picture that I will attempt to bring into focus. I will also show, in a later chapter, how these clues could be used to generate a modest prediction of where and how high the island of Atlantis was able to rise above the waves.

In this chapter, I will identify and discuss the clues that I think lead to an understanding of why Plato's claims about Atlantis should be taken seriously.

In the previous chapter, I briefly discussed the early National Science Foundation (NSF) exploration of the MAR that led to the first understanding that Alfred Wegener was right after all and that the continents do, in fact, drift apart over time. It was also discovered that the mechanism that drives that process involves a chain of upwelling plumes of magma from deep beneath the crust of the earth that ring the planet..

Now, as a result of these and other discoveries, I believe I see a pattern of clues forming that creates a basis for considering some realistic mechanisms that could very well have been responsible for creating and then destroying what would have amounted to a large island in the mid-Atlantic some eleven thousand years ago.

To explain this, I must resume discussing some of the findings of the NSF exploration of the MAR, with an emphasis on exactly how some of these findings may be clues to how Atlantis might not be a myth but an actual place in history.

As you may recall, an important aspect of the NSF exploration of the MAR involved taking core samples from the seabed at various locations to identify the type of rock that comprises the spreading centers.

The fact that the core samples taken along the ridge were riddled with pores formed by escaping gas was noted in the report of the researchers. It is not unusual to find these pores in volcanic rock; in fact, it's rather common. These pores are what make some types of volcanic rock so light that they float on water. The fact that they were found so deep in the ocean was what made them unusual.

As magma rises to the floor of the seabed from deep inside the earth, the pressures that once held dissolved gases from escaping are reduced to the point that bubbles start to form and escape the molten mass, creating vesicles, or wormholes, from the interior to the surface of the flow as it cools.

The core samples were well documented to enable the researchers to retrace the location of the cores to where they were retrieved along the ridge. What I found most interesting was the fact that cores taken from holes 10 and 11A were riddled with wormholes caused by effervescing gas. As you will see, the presence of wormholes is an indicator of how deep below sea level the lava was when it first flowed from the cracks in the seafloor.

The samples were composed of a common type of oceanic rock called basalt, formed from lava. As I've said previously, the MAR is the site of extreme volcanic activity, with molten rock almost continually flowing up from and being extruded through cracks in the hard seabed crust as lava. As the lava flows out, the pressures from below the surface are relieved, and the dissolved gases are now able to bubble out of the solution.

This is the same phenomenon we see when we open a bottle of Coke. In the soft drink, the carbon dioxide gases from which the bubbles are formed are kept dissolved within the liquid by the pressure in the bottle. When we open the bottle, the pressure is released, and we hear the swoosh sound of the escaping gas that was in the space between the liquid and the cap. With the release of pressure, the gas dissolved in the liquid effervesces out of the solution to form the bubbles characteristic of carbonated soft drinks. So, too, the lava flowing out at the surface releases its dissolved gas.

But the amount of escaping gas depends on where it reaches the surface; the lava may flow onto the ocean floor many thousands of feet below sea level. And as we all know, the deeper below the surface of the ocean, the greater the pressure. The depth of the ocean is a factor in the degree that the gas contained within the lava will effervesce. The deeper underwater the lava finds itself flowing onto the seabed, the fewer bubbles or vesicles that will be formed in it. If the lava is found at shallower depths, there will be more or even larger bubbles. As the lava solidifies, most of the gas bubbles that don't escape into the water are frozen in the rock as round bubbles and/or stringy wormholes, sort of like a freeze-frame of the bubbles in a glass of soda. There is a great advantage to this freeze-frame phenomenon for investigators, because it now provides a way to determine how deep beneath the surface of the ocean the lava was when it flowed onto the seabed floor and solidified. The size and numbers of these vesicles can be counted and measured to provide a direct gauge of how deep beneath the sea a particular sheet of lava cooled and solidified.

Here I present some quotes from the data collected by the NSF drilling activities. I noticed some telling details that made me wonder if it was beginner's luck that caused me to stumble on some of these important facts. I believe these first two clues constitute the initial evidence to unraveling the mystery of Atlantis.

The report of the Deep Sea Drilling Project by Engel and Engel (1970, 387) included the following statement: "The presence of the numerous vesicles (up to 1 centimeter in diameter) suggests either emplacement at *much shallower depths*, or different fluids and fluid pressures than commonly assumed for magmas at these depths." I inserted the italics to bring attention to the key words in the sentence. Both core sites sampled showed this same condition: a characteristic feature that would be expected from lava cooling under much lower pressures. More important to me was the fact that the samples appear to have formed in much shallower water than where they were found. In other words, the seafloor where the samples were found had sunk from the level at which the lava was first formed.

According to these findings, the MAR in this region was much more elevated at one time and much closer to the surface than it is today. This is one of many interesting clues that converge when considering the MAR as a place that has the potential of fulfilling Plato's claim of a large island existing in the Atlantic at one time in the distant past.

As I continued to examine the drilling report, I found yet another fascinating piece of data that appeared to comport with what Plato had insinuated.

Ewing and Ewing (1964); Ewing, Ewing, and Talwani (1964); Ewing, Ludwig, and Ewing (1964); and Ewing and Edgar (1966), who were investigators on the NSF study of the Deep Sea Drilling Project, all report that after studying the sediments along the ridge and the areas adjacent to the continents, there is evidence that, "Locally, however, it is clear that the sediment distribution is related to processes other than its proximity to the continental margins."

No immediate explanation is given in their review of this data. So, what interpretation can we come to? To appreciate the significance of this finding, we must understand the following: The distribution of the sediments over the ocean floor appears in different thicknesses as well as at different compositions. The ocean sediments along the edges of the continents reflect the runoff of the rivers and erosion that flow down to the sea. The sediments formed by processes that begin on the continents are called terrigenous. These are generally formed of clay and fine silt resulting from the erosion of rock and soil. They are usually thick, because the erosion of the continents by wind and rain is relatively great compared to other mechanisms that create oceanic sedimentation away from the continental margins.

The sediments that form on the ocean floor away from the continental edges result from the constant precipitation of dead animal and plant life. This creates a large portion of the sediments of oceanic origins. The ongoing decay of the sea life and the rain of organic materials onto the seafloor create this different form of sediment that geologists are easily able to distinguish. These sediments are generally referred to as pelagic.

The composition and distribution of sediment can therefore be predicted so that wherever geologists look, they can expect to find a certain type of sediment. Discovering abnormal composition and distribution is obvious to a large extent. The reports of the Ewing team (Ewing, Worzel, Ewing, and Windisch 1966; Saito et al. 1966) indicated that the distributions between the ridge and the continents were not as expected. What they did find along the MAR was a sediment distribution that more reflected what one would expect to see when studying the shores of a large island.

It is of interest to note that the ambiguous sediments were in a way "predicted" by Plato. In both the *Timaeus* and the *Critias*, he described the results of the sinking of the island of Atlantis. He interjects in the *Critias*: "When afterwards [Atlantis], sunk by an earthquake became an impassable barrier of mud to voyagers sailing from hence to any part of the ocean." And in the *Timaeus*: "For which reason the sea in those parts [where Atlantis sank] is impassable and impenetrable, because there is a shoal of mud in the way; and this was caused by the subsidence of the island."

If one reads the two passages from each dialogue, there is the suggestion that the impediment to navigation created by the sinking of Atlantis might have existed up until Plato's time. In the *Critias*, he states that the sinking caused an impassable barrier that blocked navigation "from hence to any part of the ocean," which implies that it was a problem until Plato's time. Furthermore, the passage from the *Timaeus* appears to have no ambiguity. It says that the sea in those parts *is* impassable because there *is* a shoal of mud. This clearly implies that he was discussing the current situation with that place in the ocean.

The only reason I make this point is that if the former were true, then the sinking that caused the "impassable" shoal lasted up until Plato's time. I can't find any reference to such a condition being an impediment to sailors of that time, but sailing out as far as one would have to in order to reach these shoals doesn't seem to be something that was common. Pytheas, the renowned Greek explorer from whom much of what was known of the far western coast of Europe, appeared not to venture out to sea farther than along the coastlines. As he apparently circumnavigated the British Isles and perhaps made it to Iceland, he always seemed to hug the coastlines. Was that because of the muddy shoals? I thought it an interesting question that I have been unable to verify. But considering how long ago these events transpired, it's no surprise that they are open for debate.

It's not clear why Plato would add the detail of the muddy, impassable shoals twice in separate dialogues other than that he believed it to be true. Further, it doesn't seem to otherwise support any philosophical notion, such as a utopian society or republic governing the island.

However, it does clearly serve to show that Plato wanted it to seem that he was telling a real story that now can be seen from a rational, geological point of view. I think it lends more credence to Plato's assertions about Atlantis being a historical rather than an allegorical place. He is painting a dramatic picture of that event but not an unreasonable one. He lays out details that a first historical source could have produced and would have been accepted as unalterable proof had it not occurred nine thousand years before his time.

In any case, this aspect of his claim strengthens the rationale that some geological upheaval took place at this time.

If Atlantis existed in the area of the MAR, it stands to reason that over time there would have been runoff into the sea caused by wind and rain erosion from the island. This runoff would create an uncharacteristic distribution compared to what one would expect to find as sediments, especially if one were not aware that the ridge was once above sea level. The sinking of Atlantis itself would have created an incredible disturbance. In the last years of its time, the oceans would have continually surged over the coastal areas of the island, as the rising sea levels will do to the present-day low-lying coasts if the effects of global warming come to pass. Over time, the sinking island would experience the gouging out of great quantities of the terrain that would have been washed as slurry into the surrounding waters. It would seem almost inconceivable that such an event could have occurred without some lasting sign, such as sediments that are out of place or unusually disturbed—that lasting sign is now revealed from the scientific study of the sediments at the MAR.

So far, I've touched on two pieces of evidence that point out coincidences that connect Plato to geological events of which he should have had no foreknowledge, except if they were true and passed down to him as he claims. There are several others that I'll talk about later, but it's important to first delve briefly into some of the content of Plato's works.

As I said earlier, all we know about Atlantis is found in Plato's two dialogues, *Timaeus* and *Critias*.

I think you will find that Plato's claims are compelling, especially in light of the modern understanding of the geologic structure and activity of the MAR, which provides the persuasive motivation for further investigation.

What Plato says about Atlantis involves a great deal about how the gods divided the island among the family that became the lords of the humans living there. He discusses at great length the palaces and public works that characterized the central city of Atlantis. His descriptions include details of how the buildings were constructed and how the

Atlanteans diverted hot and cold springs for the use of the populace. But these things, whether real or fabricated (as are the gods themselves), shouldn't detract from the fact that Plato asserted that the island of Atlantis was real. He admitted that the names given to the characters of the story were contrived and had been replaced with Greek names. But the concept that an island once existed and supported a fair society that became warlike over time is the bedrock of his story about Atlantis. The entire story rests on the fact that, as he claimed, the inhabitants of the island in the Atlantic Ocean once attempted to conquer the entire Mediterranean basin. And this claim, that a large island once existed in the Atlantic, is the only issue that I believe can be shown as true.

The mystery of such a place may easily have been enough to stir the imagination of the people who lived ten millennia ago and was sufficient to carry that myth up to the times of the Egyptians and in turn relate it to Plato through a family member. However, I'm not sure that there will ever be any way to produce tangible evidence to support the claim that a significant civilization lived on Atlantis as Plato intricately depicts it—certainly not including the gods and goddesses. As I mentioned previously, as Heinrich Schliemann eventually discovered, he was correct in deducing that Troy was a real place, but unlike the myth of Atlantis, Troy was mentioned in other works besides that of Homer. But it did have a basis in fact, for Troy truly did exist, despite the contemporaneous skepticism right up until it was found. A corresponding argument could be made for Plato's assertions.

It is clear that I consider Plato a serious voice, as much as scholars such as Mary Settegast (1990), an accomplished chronicler of human prehistory is, and as Schliemann saw Homer.

As I've already stated, Atlantis is mentioned in two of Plato's dialogues. In the *Critias* and *Timaeus*, Plato lays out, through narrative discussions among his associates, the entire tale of Atlantis; everything that is known about Atlantis to the present day is to be found within the pages of these two dialogues. Most of us don't realize that there is no mention of Atlantis in the historical record anywhere before this. All subsequent discussions of it are by people who lived after Plato, so there's no clear way to know if what they say has been based on what he wrote before them. And as I've also already said, Plato appears to go out of his way several times to stress that his story of Atlantis is a true one, not the kind of allegorical story he used as a tool to enhance one of his opinions or as a device to advance his lessons, as many scholars have believed. As shown in chapter 2, Plato makes this point twice, once through the character of Critias and then again through Socrates.

Consequently, if Plato meant this to be an allegory, he might not have emphasized what he insists are true accounts. He makes no such claims that any of his other allegorical works, such as *The Republic*, *Crito*, or *The Cave*, were real occurrences.

Within Plato's recounting of the story of Atlantis, he mentions several interesting evidential aspects that build on the first two pieces of evidence I mentioned earlier and that bear on the reason I was compelled to proceed with my investigation. These things, in and of themselves, should, I believe, have drawn more discussion from previous authors seeking to resolve the question of what veracity we may attribute to his claims about Atlantis. It is surprising that Plato's detractors haven't been able to dismiss several of his important assertions. Plato not only mentioned the now famous island he claimed to be larger than Libya and Asia together, which happens to be approximately the size of the raised portions of the MAR, as we will see, but also went on to make the following statement:

For in those days the Atlantic was navigable; and there was an island [Atlantis] situated in front of the straits which are by you called the Pillars of Heracles [Strait of Gibraltar today]; the island was larger than Libya and Asia [Asia Minor?] put together, and was the way to other islands, and from these you might pass to the whole of the opposite continent [North America?] which surrounded the true ocean; for this sea [Mediterranean] which is within the Straits of Heracles is only a harbour, having a narrow entrance, but that other [Atlantic Ocean] is a real sea, and the surrounding land may be most truly called a boundless continent [North America].

Evidential aspect number three: Plato's allusion to North America. As I mentioned in chapter 2, to the first settlers arriving there, North America appeared to be a boundless continent. And there is no question that it surrounds a large portion of the North Atlantic. To address Plato's comparison of this new world to the known world, considering North and South America as one continent, the two clearly dwarf Europe as it was understood in Plato's time.

I find it uncanny that within the context of a supposed fable, Plato recounted geography that would not be commonly known until the Vikings discovered North America for the "first" time over one thousand years later and wouldn't become commonly known to the Europeans for another fifteen hundred years.

The fourth piece of evidence is that Plato seems aware that the Mediterranean is much smaller than the Atlantic. That's another fact that wouldn't be known until long after Plato's time. Of course, there is that chance of coincidence, but it is still an interestingly prophetic guess, especially because he makes one amazing prediction after another.

The fifth piece of evidence, or coincidence, is where Plato placed the alleged Atlantean island of his tale and how well it corresponds to the size, situation, and shape of the MAR. If one accepts the theory that Plato was recounting a historical event, then one will need to calculate how much of the MAR would have been above sea level in order to provide enough land for the civilization he described in his dialogues. The conclusion one might come to is that Plato, once again, appeared very accurate in his recitation—and here's the reason why.

As I said earlier, the MAR is situated where Plato claimed the island of Atlantis to be, and he goes on to claim that it was "larger than Libya and Asia put together." But at first blush, this claim appears difficult to accept.

To be fair, it would have taken a significantly larger portion of the MAR above sea level than even I would be able to account for in order to equal the land *area* of Libya and Asia. However, perhaps when Plato described the size of Atlantis, he didn't mean the *area* of the island at all but more the way it looked as one approached it from the sea.

Sailing out in a westerly direction from Europe toward the MAR, the portion of it that would have been raised above sea level—representing the Atlantean island—would have been only a few hundred miles in width, east to west, at its widest point. But the east-to-west dimension would not have been observable from this point of view. However, its length north to south would have appeared to be a couple of thousand miles. Approaching the island by sea, one would have encountered an enormous land mass of unending shorelines. Consequently, because of this limited viewpoint and, ignoring how relatively narrow it was from east to west, one would unquestionably imagined that the *area* of the Atlantean island was greater than it was. Taking these ideas into account and judging by the degree of the ancients' knowledge of the dimensions of the geographic features of the world, it could very well have had the appearance of being at least as large as Libya and Asia Minor combined.

Plato goes on to make what might be considered wildly prophetic guesses, if they weren't a true recounting by those who knew, that once one traveled past the main island of Atlantis and into the open waters beyond, the journey across those waters would lead to the other side, where one would find (in Plato's words} the "opposite continent"—the Americas.

What a wonderful Jules Verne–like imagination Plato would have had to have dreamed up a story that characterized so well the real geography of the world, of which those of his time—as far as we are aware now—knew nothing. Figure 13 is a faithful copy of a nineteenth-century map originally drawn by Eratosthenes, a Greek who was so knowledgeable and capable that during Plato's time he was able to calculate the circumference of the earth to with an accuracy of 98 percent. But, despite Eratosthenes' advanced knowledge of geography, mathematics, and astronomy, his "world" map does not show North or South America.

An interesting aside: Christopher Columbus knew of Eratosthenes's measure for the circumference of the earth but used measurements made by Posidonius, a Greek philosopher who followed Eratosthenes by several centuries. Posidonius had his own calculations of the earth's circumference and concluded that the earth was smaller than Eratosthenes believed; this is why, when Columbus arrived in the West Indies, he thought he was in Asia (Freely 2013). It's a mystery why he chose the lesser of the two values for the earth's circumference. One possibility is that Columbus decided to gamble. Since nobody really knew how far the jouney would be, he decided on a distance that seemed doable.

If it was considered too far to be possible for that time, Columbus, may have not been able to raise the funding he needed. Determined that he could make the journey, he defended the shorter distance to Queen Isabella, who bought into it—literally. Meanwhile, back to what Eratosthenes did and didn't know about the world.

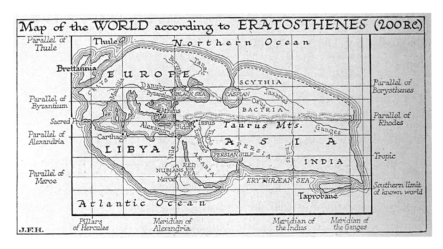

Figure 13. An early twentieth-century copy of a map originally drawn by Eratosthenes of the known world in Plato's time.

If the American continents were commonly known to any of the Greeks in Plato's time, one would have expected Eratosthenes to have known or believed it. Eratosthenes had a keen interest in geography and was able to accurately calculate the circumference of the earth. Yet he did not include the Americas in his world map. It seems very likely that the Americas weren't known to the Greeks of Plato's time, or at the very least that the existence of the Americas was not an accepted fact. In divulging this fact to his peers, Plato clearly insinuates that it was not a commonly known fact. Also, Plato adds that the very ancient Greeks did know and accepted the existence of Atlantis.

It would have been such an ancient story, even for the Greeks of Plato's time, that it may have appeared as a myth to them. To emphasize the antiquity of the Atlantis story, Plato declares that it predated the ancient Egyptians by many thousands of years. He claims at one point in the *Timaeus* that the Egyptian priests told Solon that much of Greek history was lost knowledge to his generation, and I suppose this might be an example of that historical gap. But should we believe this to be an example of Plato's vivid imagination, or did Solon really pass down the fact that there was a vast continent on the opposite side of the Atlantic from the Mediterranean?

As we have just seen in the course of relating the myth, we have a sixth piece of evidence: Plato's claims that by sailing past the islands of Atlantis, one would reach a true continent that surrounded the whole of the Atlantic Ocean, despite the understanding that there seems to be no written account by the Greeks or any peoples who lived around the Mediterranean Sea being aware of North or South America around 300 BCE, and certainly not that these continents surrounded the Atlantic, as they do. To disbelieve Plato, one is obliged to believe that it must be a coincidence and that he spun a yarn that included them: the large sunken landmass where he said Atlantis existed until it sank and that there was a vast continent opposite Europe.

My seventh piece of evidence, or coincidence, if you will, relates to the juxtaposition of when Plato claimed Atlantis sank and the geological period that included the end of the last ice age. Is it a coincidence that the geological events occurring at that time were the very ones that could have set in motion the process of lifting the MAR above sea level? Part of my argument requires a process so powerful that it could have lifted the ridge, and it seems that at the end of the last ice age, such a process existed. On that basis, I believe I can provide a scientific foundation to support the consideration of Plato's assertion.

The last ice age was a time of climatological upheaval, when the sudden rush of melting glaciers carved out the Grand Canyon and when rising oceans submerged the land bridges that connect Asia and Alaska across the Bering Strait. Along with many others, I'd always thought of the ice age as a primordial event, replete with cavemen, saber-toothed tigers, and wooly mammoths, so the possibility that Atlantis was in existence that far back makes the notion even more intriguing. So much time has passed from when Atlantis was alleged to have sunk to the present that our own civilization would have had time to evolve three times over. That would include our civilization taking its beginnings from the time of the pyramid-building Egyptians. Three times the age of our civilization is so long ago that the physical trail leading to Atlantis is as cold as the ice age into which it may have vanished. As long ago as that seems, there is evidence that humans have carried on some aspects of civilization during what we have commonly considered the Stone Age, or Pleistocene.

It has been hypothesized most recently, and with strong geologic evidence, that the Great Sphinx of Egypt is far older than has previously been thought. The new estimates for its original construction, made by Boston University geologist Robert Schoch (2000), date it to between 7,000 and 5,000 BCE. Schoch examined the erosion patterns of the Sphinx's paws and legs and found them to be inconsistent with presently accepted estimates. His analysis determined that despite the commonly accepted theory that the erosion on the sides of the Sphinx was most likely due to blowing sand, there is evidence that it was caused by the action of water. This leads him to believe that the Sphinx could only have been constructed and have existed during the time when northern Africa was wet with sufficient running water. He also determined the age by other chemical reaction products that he believes support his hypothesis.

There have been academic challenges made by archaeologists and Egyptologists opposing Schoch's theory that rest largely on their demand that the pro-water erosion proponents demonstrate the existence of a contemporary civilization to support such a monumental engineering feat. The arguments against an earlier dating than Egyptologists commonly accept for the Great Sphinx have been successful because evidence for contemporary civilization to match the earlier dating had been largely absent.

But in other parts of the world, there *is* such contemporary evidence, which predates even the earliest construction dates for the Sphinx. Now, in defense of Schoch, an early stone monolith–building civilization has been discovered in present-day Turkey in an area known as Gobekli Tepe, among ruins that have been carbon-dated to around 11,000 BCE (see figure 14). The structures are more complex than Stonehenge, incorporating monoliths on which are found intricate carvings of animals. In that regard, the hypothesis proposed by Schoch may have more validity than first supposed; the argument proposed by detractors that no contemporary civilization existed as far back as he calculates for the Great Sphinx is answered by the monolithic structures at Gobekli Tepe. So it seems that there were people capable of some aspects of complex monolithic constructions associated with a civilization as far back as the Upper Paleolithic, the Stone Age. In the artist's depiction from National Geographics of one of these archaeological sites (see figure 15), one is struck by the industry and organization required to accomplish such an amazing feat of construction.

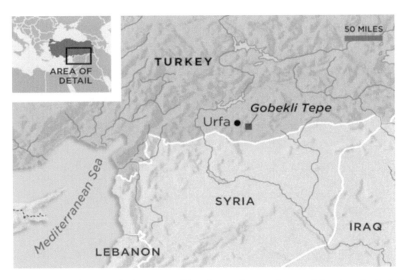

Figure 14. Map showing the location of the eleven-thousand-year-old archaeological site of Gobekli Tepe – the same period claimed by Plato for Atlantis.

Figure 15. Artist's rendering (National Geographics) of the Gobekli Tepe excavation site in Turkey depicting the complexity of this Paleolithic structure as it may have appeared under construction, clearly at odds with all accepted understanding of what Stone Age cultures were capable of creating.

The carving on the twenty-foot-high stele (see figure 16) would by itself have been a remarkable find for the time, but in concert with the intricate architectural layout, the picture of an enormously capable people begins to emerge, in stark contrast to what was commonly believed of those living in those times.

Figure 16. One of many columns unearthed at a sprawling site in Gobekli Tepe, Turkey, estimated to be eleven thousand years old.

It has recently been reported by researchers that domestication of grains was begun at least twenty-three thousand years ago along the shores of the Sea of Galilee—thousands of years earlier than had previously been believed (Snir et al. 2015). This implies that during the time Plato sets out for the existence of Atlantis, humans had begun to develop agriculture. This was a turning point for humanity that enabled the feeding of a larger population and the division of labor into hunters, arrowhead makers, herdsmen, and so forth, allowing for permanent settlements and time for other endeavors besides just hunting and gathering.

It now appears that there are several supporting discoveries that push back the time frame in which humans were more greatly organized than previously believed and capable of building large stone structures. We've now learned that there is reason to believe that the Sphinx may be thousands of years older than originally predicted, that the Gobekli Tepe monolithic site is estimated to be at least eleven thousand years old, and that humans were cultivating grains twenty-three thousand years ago.

Realizing that so much was going on much further back in time than we had ever expected contributes additional compelling evidence that there may be some truth to the Atlantis myth after all, and the entire work of figuring out how it might have been possible no longer seems such a fool's errand.

Despite the well-formulated argument against Atlantis laid out by dozens of skeptical scholars, including writers for the magazine *Skeptical Inquirer*, the supporting evidence may finally be at hand. I happen to be a strong proponent of the *Skeptical Inquirer* and can understand how they can disparage belief in the Atlantis myth. Kevin Christopher, writing in the *Skeptical Inquirer*, points to the fact that we have no evidence that anyone except Plato knew of this spectacular chapter in Greek history. But as an argument, it only begs the question of what's not known about Greek history. Christopher inaccurately states in the same article that no civilization had been found as far back as eleven thousand years ago. But there was such a civilization, as we have seen in Gobekli Tepe. Further, the *Skeptical Inquirer* asserts that those who choose to place Atlantis anywhere else but in the Atlantic Ocean are immediately presenting a losing argument. Anywhere but the Atlantic significantly changes Plato's story—he went to great lengths to describe its location in the Atlantic Ocean. Of course, that is exactly where I am going to show that it existed. Writing for the website Live Science, Benjamin Radford (2018) adds that "Plato made up Atlantis as a plot device for his stories . . . because there were no other records of it anywhere else in the world." Writing for *National Geographic*, Willie Drye (n.d.) quotes James Room, a professor of classics at Bard College in Annandale, New York, as saying, "It's a story that captures the imagination . . . It's a great myth. It has a lot of elements that people love to fantasize about." Many people would agree, but these are not substantive arguments.

And just as it seems that the greatest of Plato's claims is impossible to confirm, a new view of the geological events that occurred in the frigid days of the Pleistocene, the last ice age, appear to have some significant credibility. These new geologic possibilities would put important aspects of what we believe we know about neolithic history into question.

The next chapter will explore the chain of events that would have been required for Plato to be redeemed once and for all. There is now real evidence that is not in the form of wild hand-waving or smoke and mirrors but solid, logical argument with geological backing.

CHAPTER 6
ICE AGE CHAIN REACTION:
THE RISE OF ATLANTIS

In the previous chapters, we've examined the preliminaries and background of the Atlantis myth and the geological primers concerning the place Plato claimed it to be. Now it's time to get down to explaining how all these things tie together and how it's possible for what some claim to be impossible to have occurred. This chapter offers the details of the hypothesis that I believe provides irrefutable support for Plato's assertions—namely, that in the chilling grip of the ice age, a large island with a mild climate, which he called Atlantis, lay in the Atlantic Ocean but no longer exists today.

The foundation for my argument concerns a chain of events that occurred during the Pleistocene. Although there were many ice ages, the one of concern was the last and that I contend created the circumstances that caused the MAR to rise to historic heights. Plato went on to claim that Atlantis provided an island for an ancient civilization off the coast of the Iberian Peninsula.

The hypothesis as stated in this book is based on well-known and accepted geological principles and phenomena that are enumerated next so that it's clear to see that this is not a hocus-pocus, smoke-and-mirrors proposition. We have strong evidence that, in the last ice age,

- the oceans were lower by at least 420 feet, or 130 meters;

- the glaciers caused Iceland's crust to sink more than fifteen hundred feet;

- Icelandic volcanoes were buried and the hot spot magma flows diverted by the glaciers;

- Icelandic magma found a southward path to the MAR;

- the Icelandic crust rose back up after the glaciers melted;

- the MAR has always been much higher than the rest of the ocean basin; and

- the ocean seafloors rise and fall with changes in sea levels.

With what is already known in the literature of the dynamics of postglacial rebound of the earth's crust in North America, Europe, and Iceland, we can make some first order-of-magnitude estimates about how much of a rise the MAR could have experienced under these interrelated circumstances.

As far back as the 1800s, after Agassiz first proposed the concept of ice ages, scientists have speculated on the effect that these glaciers would have on the crust of the earth. In 1882, T. F. Jamieson wrote, according to Christensen (312), "I suggested that the enormous weight of ice laid upon the surface of the country might have caused a depression, while the melting of the ice would also account for the rising again of the land."

To frame this discussion, let's look at what was going on during the last ice age, when men were learning to paint beautiful ochre and charcoal renderings of bison and mammoths on cave walls, hunting wooly rhinos with stone-tipped spears, and warding off saber-toothed tigers with torches of bundled reeds.

During the Upper Pleistocene, in the beginning of the last ice age, in a period known as the Wisconsin Glaciations, vast areas of the northern tiers of most of the Northern Hemisphere were covered in those glaciers.

These were not just the kind of glaciers we're used to seeing in travelogues, which wend their way down the narrow, picturesque mountain passes of the Rockies or Alps. These glaciers spread laterally hundreds and even thousands of miles across the continents, towering thousands of feet above the surrounding landscape at their leading edge.

The vast woodland and prairie terrains of continents in the Northern Hemisphere were transformed into icy, barren, inhospitable landscapes. They were frozen over for thousands of years, with only momentary breaks of warming that did little to create the long-in-coming meltdown. That meltdown didn't arrive all at once but over thousands of years and, according to the National Oceanic and Atmospheric Administration, was more or less complete by around eleven thousand years ago—coincidentally, exactly when Plato said Atlantis sank.

These glaciers left their mark on the continents in the obvious carving of the landscape as mountain valleys, finger lakes, and detritus deposits. They also built moraines (hills plowed up in front of the glaciers) such as the long, parallel hills of the Midwest and in places like Long Island, but in other less obvious ways. They left the crusts of the continent slumped down from the enormous weight of the former burden of ice and are still very slowly rising back to their original elevation, to this day.

The glaciers were a result of one of the basic natural cycles going awry—the water cycle. What we learned about the water cycle in junior high was that rain and snow are formed indirectly from evaporated water. The evaporation occurs as the sun shines on the earth and heats the ponds, lakes, and oceans. That vaporized water rises into the atmosphere to become clouds. Eventually, the microscopic water vapor particles of the clouds condense around the dust and bacteria (yes, bacteria) floating in the atmosphere. When enough water droplets coalesce and become too heavy, they fall back to earth as precipitation. The runoff of rains become streams and rivers that sooner or later make it back to the lakes and oceans to start the cycle all over again.

This water cycle is a continuing process in warm climatic times. But in the case of ices ages, the normal water cycle is broken. When the global climate is not warm enough in the summer to melt all the snow that has fallen the previous winter, the small amount that remains each year in higher elevations builds up as ever-thickening snowpacks and, eventually, into glaciers. So, it's not how cold it gets in the winter but how warm it doesn't get in the summer.

When the snow of subsequent winters begins to build, it becomes impacted by the weight of ever-increasing snowfalls, eventually forming into ice, much as a snowball does if we squeeze it tightly enough in our gloved hands. Glaciers form in normal climatic times in the high elevations of mountains. Today we see them melting or receding, which appears to indicate the beginning of a new climatic cycle.

During the onset of the last ice age, glaciers formed over the northern tiers of Asia, Europe, and North America 2.6 million years ago (see figure 17). During this period, there were several glaciations that formed, then melted, and formed again to some degree or another. At times they grew to be thousands of feet above the surrounding terrain, and not only in the high elevations of mountains. The glaciers also spilled out onto the plains in front of mountain ranges, creating dramatic walls of ice. Summoning the image of the ice wall from *Game of Thrones* would be a wonderful illustration of how they may have appeared.

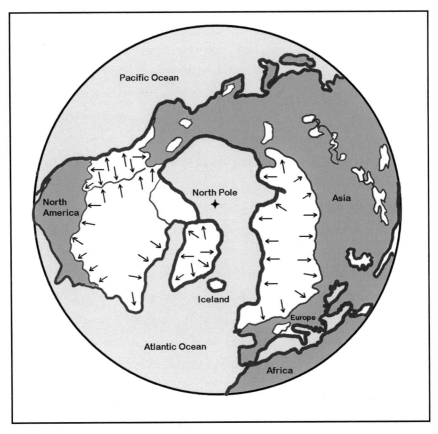

Figure 17. A polar view of the glacier patterns across the Northern Hemisphere during the last ice age (approx. 17kyr bp). Arrows indicate direction of spreading.

The recent glacial periods appear to follow a one-hundred-thousand-year period, though the causality is yet unproven. However, according to a favorite hypothesis of geologists, there is a so-called Croll/Milankovitch cycle, which is based on the theory that the motions of the earth are contributors to the glaciations that occur on these reoccurring intervals. The earth has several features of its rotation and orbit that are believed to affect the amount of solar insolation, or the amount of sunlight that falls on the earth. Scientists have in fact been able to collect strong evidence that the glacial cycles are related to the motions of the earth and its orbit.

In recent times, the glacial cycles have been associated with the tilt of the earth's axis—which accounts for the variations in the amount of solar heating.

The reason that the tilt of the earth's axis affects the amount of ice that builds up at the poles is a consequence of the amount of atmosphere that the light has to travel through to reach the ground and how a low angle stretches the light over a larger area, reducing its intensity per unit area. As an example, in the first diagram in figure 18 of the tilt of the earth's axis, the north-south axis is tilted toward the sun. The second diagram depicts the north-south axis tilted away from the sun, as it was eleven thousand years ago. In the first diagram, the sun's rays travel through a short distance of atmosphere; in the second, the rays must travel a greater distance to reach the ground. The light reaching the ground goes – in the first illustration – from a circle to the second where it is spread to a larger oval. Therefore, the sun's rays are absorbed as they travel through the atmosphere, and the more atmosphere they traverse, the more they are absorbed and less of the sun's energy reaches the surface, as well as diffusing over a greater area.

During the ice ages, it is believed that the extreme tilt of the earth's axis contributed to the building of the glaciers due to less sunlight reaching the northern latitudes. The reason the earth's axis changes is related to a wobble in its spin that may be caused by changes in the rate at which it rotates. When ice skaters spin, they can decrease their spinning speed by extending their arms away from their body. Imagine a spinning toy top—it spins straight up and down like a skater. As it slows, it begins to wobble, causing it to eventually tip, and its axis of rotation begins to make circles. Changes inside the earth and with continental drift seem to be analogous and can influence the tilt of the earth's axis.

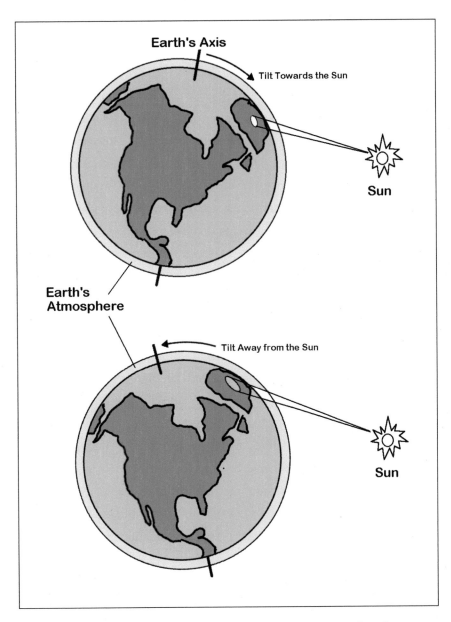

Figure 18. The diagrams above Illustrate how the tilt of the earth's axis affects the warming or cooling of the Earth. When the axis tilts away from the sun a given point on the surface cools because the path for rays through the atmosphere is longer and more spread out.

Also, if the tilt of the axis was very small, or if the earth's axis was straight up and down with no tilt, there would be little variation in the seasons. If the tilt was very much exaggerated, the poles would tilt much more toward the sun and there would be a melting of the poles, rising sea levels, global warming, and great cyclical changes in the seasons.

Two million years ago, there was a very good match for a forty-one-thousand-year cycle of glaciers building and receding. However, over the last million years, there was a distinct hundred-thousand-year event cycle of glaciation, with a poor association with a solar insolation cycle. But whatever the mechanisms that force the earth into periods of glacial expansion and recession, the chain of events that we are going to follow started around one hundred ten thousand years ago, the most recent period that glaciation began.

Over the last twenty-two thousand years, since the height of the last glaciation, the global sea level has risen by 420 feet, or 130 meters. However, Donald Prothero, a well-respected world-famous geologist, along with a colleague, estimated an even greater rise than previously believed and concluded that the oceans have risen substantially more. Prothero wrote, "During warmer interglacial periods, melting ice releases water and causes a rise in sea level. Analyses of Pleistocene ice-water budgets suggest that the net global sea level could fluctuate by roughly 150 m" (Prothero and Schwab 1996, 272). One hundred fifty meters is almost five hundred feet. Since the oceans have risen considerably since the last ice age, it is obvious that they had been that much lower. The location of today's seaport cities would have been hundreds of miles from the sea during these periods when the sea levels had dropped so drastically. The continental shelf we see on maps of the ocean's depth (usually the lighter blue areas adjacent to the coastlines) around North America depict an ancient coastline that extends far out into what today is ocean. Low lying places, such as Florida would have had much more land area as a result.

Though it may take thousands of years, the lowered sea-level effect becomes an unbalancing geological mechanism. The enormous amount of water evaporated from the oceans was locked up in the glacial ice that bore the enormous burden of weight on the continents over which they had built up. And as we have learned, the weight of the glaciers depressed the bedrock hundreds and even thousands of feet under it. The sinking, or in geological terms, the subsistence, resulted in considerable reduction in the elevation of the crust under all the glacier-covered land of the Northern Hemisphere. The melting of the glaciers not only caused the sea levels to rise once again but also allowed the continental crust to rise back to its original elevation.

In an area of Scandinavia and a portion of Finland known as Fennoscandia, the land continues the process of rebounding upward as a result of the glacial recession. The rebound occurring after the melting of the glaciers' almost unbearable burden is much like how a rowboat bobs back up as a person steps from it onto a dock, but the crustal rebound process occurs much, much more slowly. Whereas the rowboat bobs back up immediately, the earth's crust rebounds in a time scale on the order of thousands and even hundreds of thousands of years.

The Icelandic island was pushed downward in sort of a saucer-shaped, bending pattern; in the process, the asthenosphere—the pliant layer of the earth below the hard crust—was pushed aside. When the glaciers finally melted, the weight was lifted from the crust, and the asthenosphere flowed back and began the process of uplifting the crust to its original height. The flow of the asthenosphere accounts for part of the overall rebound or uplift of the crust when the weight of the glacier is removed. The balance of the rebound phenomena is from the crust itself. The crustal component of rebound is much quicker than the slower flow of the asthenosphere, even though the crust is considerably more rigid.

The mechanism responsible for the crustal rebound is a phenomenon called flexural rigidity. Flexural rigidity is the characteristic of materials associated with the degree to which they bend when flexed under a given load, a subject that has been explained and investigated by many geologists, including Fjeldskaar (1997).

The crust can bend, much as a diving board does when stepped on. Imagine watching a slow-motion sequence of a diver jumping off a diving board. You would be able to see the board slowly spring back to its original position. After the crust is subjected to bending, it also springs back. The amount of springing back of the diving board or the crust is also a function of thickness. A thin diving board would be more easily bent, allowing it to bend back and forth more easily. Likewise, a thin versus a thick crust would react accordingly.

Flexural rigidity is a characteristic of the crust that works with a broader phenomenon—isostatic compensation. The interaction of the floating crust on the asthenosphere is the isostatic compensation effect (also called isostasy). Though flexural rigidity and isostasy are independent of each other, these phenomena very often act simultaneously. The process by which the earth's crust is subsided by the glaciers and the subsequent rebound can be estimated by geologists by calculating the isostatic compensation, or isostasy.

The concept behind isostasy was first developed and described by the Greek mathematician Archimedes around twenty-two hundred years ago. His famous bathtub epiphany was supposed to illustrate the principle of buoyancy by demonstrating that as he lowered himself into his tub, the volume of water that was displaced was equal to the volume of his body. According to Archimedes, an object floats on a liquid because it weighs less than the volume of water it displaces. When we look at an enormous cruise ship and wonder how it floats, we are faced with the counterintuitive phenomenon of buoyancy. But the ship floats for the same reason Archimedes discovered—the water it pushes aside weighs more than the ship itself.

Yet even though scientists understand the buoyancy aspect of isostasy, there are several current theories to explain isostasy that arrive at different real-world results. Two leading theories were developed in the 1800s, one by Sir George Airy and the other by John Henry Pratt. They were originally created to understand why mountain ranges stand high above plains and why plains seem to be slumping crust. It's unclear whether mountains are higher because they are made of less dense rock or whether there's just more rock piled up over the underlying asthenosphere. According to our ship analogy, how high or low the ship rides in the water might be a result of either how much cargo is piled up on the decks or whether the ship is constructed of many fewer internal open cabin spaces.

However, for the sake of this discussion, it doesn't really matter which model we consider because the intensity of the rising magma convection cells at play under the MAR are far more influential than the weaker isostatic forces operating alone far from the spreading centers. For example, the ocean basin crusts sink to an equilibrium level, according to theory, because of the balance between their density, the water column above them, and the restoring forces of isostasy on them. But the forces under the MAR are not only a result of the isostatic force but also due to the overwhelming forces of the rising convection plume at the spreading center.

In our quest to draw some rough estimates of how high the MAR can rise, we need to disentangle the relevant forces. We can start to do this by sorting out what the result is for the present and what it should have been eleven thousand years ago, during the time Plato claims a large island existed in the Atlantic.

The geophysical processes occurring along the mid-ocean ridges are understood from an empirical point of view; what is known is a result of what is observed but not what is completely understood or predictable. As we can see from the different models of isostasy, there are various opinions about some of the subtlest aspects of what is going on under the crust. But there are fundamental facts from observation about the crust of the earth that are understood with confidence—things such as that the weight of the glaciers subsides and deforms the crust and that, after the glaciers melt, the crust rises again to its original level. There are ways to calculate how loads on structures bend them and their reaction to being subjected to loading. These are things we know from constructing bridges and buildings. What is happening miles below the crust is known mostly from the data collected from remote-sensing devices.

The sensing and measuring instrumentation available to geologists today has provided an abundance of data but less information about the actual mechanisms on which they are collecting data. Mathematics is the tool that provides the modeling competency for offering rough estimates of what to expect if one thing happens after another but not necessarily to the extent, in many cases, of how much and how fast; much of geology is not an exact science, sort of like weather forecasting. In meteorology, there's the American model and the European model, as well as others that offer explanations of hurricane tracks, yet with different results and sometimes with substantive variances. The contending views about a lot of geology and geophysics are based on trying to fit the data to a working theory. I suppose in some sense, one could consider me to be following the conventional path by proposing a theory that fits existing data to observations, leading to a conclusion.

As seawater evaporated from the ocean basins and fell as snow, to become glaciers, the sea levels began to drop dramatically. As I mentioned earlier, there was a drop in sea level of at least 420 feet, or 130 meters, during those periods. According to Frederikse, Riva, and King (2017), the height of sea level influences the elevation of the seafloor under it.

Because so much water weight was removed from the oceanic crust, the seafloor began to rise. We saw that Iceland and Fennoscandia are undergoing that today in their postglacial rebound period. If we apply the rebound process to the MAR, we would expect lowered sea levels to cause an associated rebound, or rise, in the oceanic floor crust. How much the oceanic crust would be expected to rise depends on what factors are considered as controlling influences. In the case of the MAR, there is the additional consideration of the spreading center plume.

To determine what degree of rebound can occur at the MAR, we need to examine the nature of the ocean basins both near and at a distance from it. The ocean basins plunge to nearly eighteen thousand feet below sea level between Africa and the MAR, according to Google Earth, which has been validated for accuracy by Rusli et al. (2014). The seafloors in the particular areas of the spreading centers which we will be concerned with, (the Azores Plateau) have a depth of about six thousand feet, or eighteen-hundred meters, below the surface, on average. This is a shallower depth than the average MAR range, which is around eight-thousand feet. As we've discussed, the mid-ocean ridges are elevated due to the upwelling of enormous plumes of magma. If this thermal geologic conveyor belt at the spreading centers was to cease, the ridge would sink to the level of the other oceanic crusts east and west of it, and the oceans would have smooth-bottomed seafloors throughout, like the bottom of a bathtub.

But, of course, the ridges are there, and in the North Atlantic, areas adjacent to the MAR rise above sea level in several of those few points around the Azores. The Azores are mere dots in the Atlantic, where the seafloor crust reaches the surface. The remainder of the Atlantic basin away from the ridge doesn't come anywhere near the surface. It's clear that the power of the spreading center is the force that keeps the MAR well above the rest of the seafloor. If the Atlantic were drained, then standing at the bottom of the empty ocean basin and looking toward the crest of the MAR, one would see a mountain range as great in height as the Rockies.

Interestingly, the MAR is the highest of all earth's oceanic spreading centers. Why the MAR is so much higher than the rest of the spreading centers that girdle the earth and rise above the surrounding ocean basins is a good question. The question then becomes: Is there more than one discrete force at work at the MAR, and if so, how can we quantify those forces in a meaningful way? To do that, we need to break down the individual forces at play by the fraction of what they contribute to the normal uplift and rebound phenomenon caused by the lowered sea levels.

The MAR is composed of a similar density crust as the rest of the seafloor and should otherwise sink if it weren't for the spreading center plume. It appears that the density of the MAR crust is a factor we can ignore.

Considering the depth of the ocean basins—nearly eighteen thousand feet—and the average depth of the MAR—six thousand feet—we can see with basic math that the forces under the MAR are able to raise it at least three times as high as those under the rest of the ocean basins:

18,000 feet ÷ 6,000 feet = 3

or, from another perspective, a ratio of 3:1

Another fact is that the Azores that straddle the MAR are above a hot spot. The status of this hot spot is debated, but looking at the nearby MAR, the hot spot is obviously contributing some extra elevation to the oceanic crust in that region.

So, what does this all mean? In the simplest terms, it means that we have a starting point from which to begin an estimate of how high the MAR could rise to comport with Plato's claims.

Let's see what other clues we can tease out. The crust of one side of the MAR is moving away from the crust of the other side (by definition, it is at a spreading center). Then it is apparent that the crust of the MAR is divided—in fact, it is part of two different diverging plates in the earth's crust. The enormous plume rising from deep inside the earth is pushing out at this weak and fractured point in the crust. An analogy would be how easy it is to push your finger through a piece of paper with a slit cut in it rather than with no slit. The crust around the spreading centers and, in particular, the MAR is much more flexible than anywhere else in the seafloor.

Understanding the structure of the MAR and why it's different from the surrounding seafloors and the continental crusts will help us understand how and why it is subject to the dramatic changes that I'm suggesting it goes through.

The thickness of the continents averages between twenty-five to forty miles. The seafloors, on the other hand, are only a few miles thick—from one to five miles and about seven miles around the Azores. The crust of the MAR is part of the ocean basins, except that it is greatly elevated by the spreading center plumes. But the crust of the MAR is still only a few miles thick.

Thinking back to how the glaciers pushed the continents down thousands of feet under their weight, and keeping in mind that those continents are over twenty miles thick, the seafloor crust is subject to bigger displacements than its thicker cousins. The ocean waters pushed down the seafloors in a similar manner that the glaciers do to the continental crust, but the seafloors are much thinner and are pushed down more easily.

The seafloor is composed of rock that is denser than that of the continents. The denser seafloor rock sinks more easily. However, the seafloor is so much thinner that the density difference is negligible. Because water seeks its own level, the deeper parts of the seafloor gather more water until an equilibrium is attained. And just as the continents sag under the weight of the glaciers, so do the seafloors sag under the weight of the oceans.

But it is apparent that the converse is true; the enormous rising magma plumes easily push up the thin crust of the seafloor. The MAR is such a place. It is possible that small, otherwise unmeasurable changes in the volume of magma rising under the MAR could quickly make measurable changes to the height of the thin ocean crust.

It is obvious that the forces under the MAR are three times as strong as the normalizing forces under the rest of the ocean. We know that from the difference in elevation of the MAR and the ocean basins in general.

Let's try to use some of what we've just discussed to start building an estimate of how high the MAR could ever rise. To begin with, we know about the rebound effect, such as how the continental crust is rising back from being subsided by the glaciers. Let's apply that to the MAR, for when the glaciers were building, the oceans were lowering. The weight removed from the seafloor should have caused the seafloor to rise, especially around the MAR, which was already elevated and has a more flexible crust with the "slit" in it.

As soon as the ocean levels dropped, the seafloor would naturally begin to rise back to the prior level.

Using a standard equation from an example in a well-worn geology go-to tome, *Mechanics in the Earth and Environmental Sciences* (1994) by Middleton and Wilcock, I calculated the amount of rebound, or uplift, the ridge should experience as a result of the oceans being lowered by about 420 feet (the average of the leading ocean rise/lowering data I presented earlier). Middleton and Wilcock find that the crust under a glacier is subsided about one-third the thickness of the glacier. The rebound is the same. For the seafloor, the rise could be one-third of the 420-foot drop in sea level, or about 140 feet.

This result makes it look as though the possibility of the ridge ever rising much above sea level very unlikely. For someone looking for the MAR to rise above sea level, it isn't much at all because the MAR is thousands of feet below sea level. But this was my initial calculation before I realized that I hadn't considered all the factors I should have. And, of course, the calculations just mentioned would not create much of an island—certainly not one with the extent depicted by Plato.

However, as I discussed previously, the MAR already stands much higher above the rest of the Atlantic Ocean floor, so the reason for this condition must be factored into the calculation. Therefore, in order to properly calculate the degree the MAR could have risen, we also must add in the upward force imparted by the magmatic convection current under the spreading center. We can see from the evaluation the difference between the amounts the ocean basins are subsided and how much less the MAR is pushed down; we already noted that difference factor of about 3:1 (not to be confused with the 3:1 isostatic rebound).

So, because of the lowering of the oceans, the MAR should have risen about 140 feet from isostasy alone. But we need to include the additional height adjustment from the spreading center convection current plume. The isostatic rise, plus three times that from the convection plume, could have propelled it 420 feet ($3 \times 140 = 420$).

We're still not done with factoring in what we know. If we digress and forget about all these forces like isostasy and others we've discussed, the sea level would have dropped 420 feet. If you lived along a coastline during that time, the sea level along the shore would have dropped 420 feet. We will have to include the sea level dropping 420 feet in our calculation for the MAR. Now we can expect a total apparent rise of up to about 840 feet. As big a rise as 840 feet might seem, the MAR and the Azores Plateau are typically six thousand feet below sea level. At that rate, not much of either would be above sea level. Yes, there would have been an island or islands that were bigger than the current area of the Azores, but it would hardly have created the large island for which we're looking. We seem to be headed in the right direction, though.

As it is, there are more aspects of the forces around the Azores Plateau that form the highest points around the MAR. The reaction of the oceanic crust, by the nature of its structure and dimensions, will be vastly different from what we observe for the continental crust, and we'll soon see why. Also, we haven't discussed the consequences of the fact that the crust of the spreading centers, in contrast to the rest of the ocean basin, is articulated; I'll explain more about that in a moment.

Now, in order to show how the MAR rose still farther than what we've seen, I'll need to introduce yet another aspect of a force that was present to bring the MAR high enough above sea level to create the large island predicted by Plato.

To introduce the next aspect of the MAR rise, we need to look back to the processes that were ongoing during the last ice age. That last ice age didn't just lower the sea levels and cause the isostatic rise in the seafloor. The glaciers created another and entirely different chain of events.

It's of interest and importance that we are concerned with the glaciers covering Iceland because of its proximity to the MAR, and here is the reason why.

Iceland is situated directly over the same spreading center that swells the MAR. Iceland is also situated above a hot spot—one of the most active on the planet. During the last ice age, as glaciers spread across the Northern Hemisphere, they capped off the Icelandic volcanoes that serve as the vents for the hot spot above which the island is situated. The hot spot plumes are rising blobs of magma, very much like the blobs in a lava lamp. They are different from the spreading center's magma that wells up along the ridgelines that ring the planet in "sheets" of a convection current. As for the hot spot plumes, their cause is not well understood but we see them in other places around the world, such as under the Hawaiian Islands and in Yellowstone National Park. One recently was discovered under Italy, and there are others under Iceland and the Azores.

The hot spot under Iceland, which is an extraordinary upwelling of magma, has caused the island to rise far above sea level, very much the way another hot spot has caused the Hawaiian Islands to rise in the Pacific. By building a volcanic seamount of cooled lava and a plume of hot magma, the Hawaiian Islands are a combination of basaltic rock, and physically uplifted crust that are buoyed by the plume. In the case of Hawaii, the plate on which the islands rest is moving relative to that hot spot. So, the plume of magma breaks through the crust and builds a small island. But over time, the crust moves, and when it's far enough beyond the plume, the hot spot can no longer easily reach the original path upward to the crust. Subsequently, a new island begins to be created as the plume breaks through a new piece of the moving oceanic crust. However, because the hot spot feeding Iceland sits directly beneath the MAR spreading center, the plume has an unchanging path to the surface and the island continually accumulates new basaltic rock over tens of millions of years.

During the last ice age, glaciers on Iceland amassed to a height of about six thousand feet, or eighteen hundred meters, causing the central plain of the island to sink sixteen hundred feet, or five hundred meters, according to Sigmundsson (2006). The rebound—the uplifting of the island to its original height after the glaciers melted—took only about one thousand years, according to the same researcher at the Nordic Volcanological Center in Reykjavik, Iceland. That is an incredibly rapid rebound, since most usually occur over many millennia, so by any standard it points to how rapidly some of the events surrounding the rise and fall of the crust of the spreading centers and the MAR may also occur. This effect will also, not surprisingly, play a role in the myth about Atlantis.

There is another aspect to the glacial buildup on Iceland that relates to the connection between the timing of the ice age and the rise of the MAR and the nearby Azores Plateau. When the glaciers capped off Iceland's volcanoes the supply of magma directly beneath the Icelandic island was cut off. But that couldn't stop the constant, enormous volcanic buildup and activity generating the plume below Iceland in its relentless rise—the capped-off magma had to go somewhere else, and it did.

In my research, I came upon an interesting paper that described the same event we're discussing regarding the capping of the Icelandic hot spot plume. According to the *Scientific American* article "The Earth's Hot Spots" by Vink, Morgan, and Vogt (1985), it is possible for a hot spot to feed a ridge from a distance, where the plume is either blocked or just finds a new, more relatively elevated path of least resistance to the surface (see figure 19).

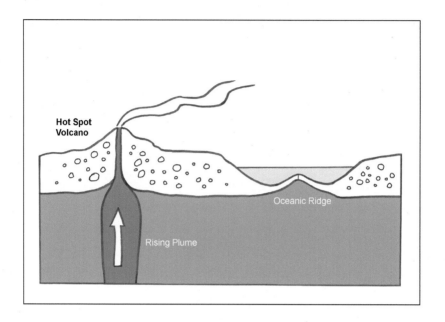

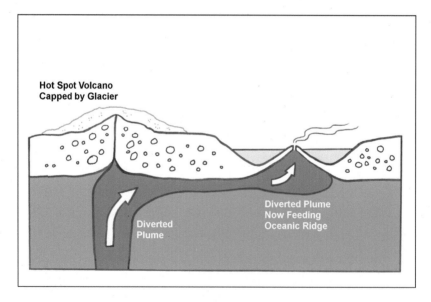

Figure 19. A hot spot feeding an oceanic ridge, modeled after Vink, Morgan, and Vogt (1985). A hot spot volcano is located near a spreading center (first panel). Glaciers cap the volcanic flow (second panel), and the weight lowers its elevation, diverting the magma toward the higher elevation at the spreading center.

An examination of a bathymetric map of the Atlantic (see figure **20**) shows the extraordinary telltale sign of how the capped-off hot spot plume under Iceland at one time migrated southwardly, down and along the MAR crest.

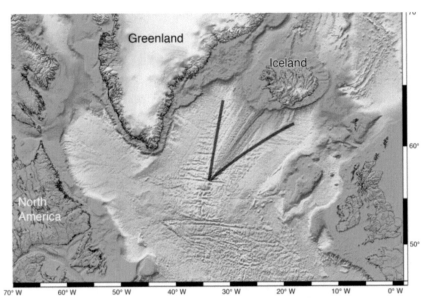

Figure 20. The V-shaped layering left by the migrating plume under Iceland. The arrowhead is added to show the direction to the MAR and the extent of the magma excursion (NOAA satellite survey).

The evidence of this phenomenon is a V-shaped layering of the southern edge of the Icelandic Plateau on which Iceland rests, literally forming an arrowhead pointing south toward the most elevated portion of the MAR and the Azores Plateau—and perhaps at one time to Atlantis?

It was also discovered, according to Vink et al. (1985), that the Icelandic plume migration hasn't been a consistent, constant flow but has been occurring over time in "pulses" of unknown causality. That is to say, the reason for the occasional bursts of additional magma flowing down the margin of the MAR is not understood, and though several candidate processes have been suggested, there isn't one on which geologists who study Iceland can agree.

It is clear, according to Vink et al. (1985), that as a result of the capping-off effect of the Icelandic volcanic calderas (see figure 21, which shows the focus of the plume under the Vatnajökull volcano), the hot magma plume under the island began to migrate southward toward the spreading center to the south. The reason the plume diverted south along the spreading center ridgeline, according to Vink and colleagues' assertion, was that the ridgeline was elevated relative to the Icelandic Plateau. The plume of hot magma, seeking a route along which to rise, followed the path of least resistance.

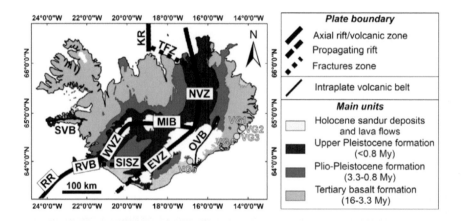

Figure 21. *Three active rift zones: the northern, the western, and the eastern zones. The center of the hot spot plume is identified in the eastern triple junction zone as OVB (Federico Pasquaré Mariotto andFabio Luca Bonali: (© Department of Human and Innovation Sciences, Insubria University, Via S. Abbondio 12, 22100 Como, Italy.)*

The plume then assumed its southerly flow along the crest of the MAR, moving inexorably toward the area of the Azores Plateau, which we know is the most elevated portion of the spreading center ridgeline. The only thing in the way of the plume would have been a transform fault that connects to the ridge crest to the south by the Charlie-Gibbs Fracture Zone that runs for about one hundred miles east to west. The ridgeline along which the plume was flowing had shifted to the west by about one hundred miles during this period.

However, if the crust was elevated relative to the Icelandic Plateau, and due to the enormous pressure created by hot spot plumes, it would have followed the features of this obstacle and again found its way back under the central parts of the MAR. At the bottom of the V formation that denotes the Icelandic plume diversion point, there appears to be some irregular crustal thickening, which is seen again at the continuation of the southward MAR ridge crest. It would seem that where the V formation encountered the transform fault, there was a period where the magma backed up and caused the crustal thickening. Because it could not go backward, the way for it to flow was along the fault until it encountered the continuation of the ridge crest. Once again, it stalled before flowing upward toward the Azores Plateau.

If the Icelandic hot spot plume had stalled at the transform fault, we should have seen the evidence of this as a massive thickening of the crust at that intersection, much as at the V-shaped Reykjanes Ridge. But we don't, which supports my case that it continued to find its way along the fault line, back to the crest of the MAR (see figure 22).

Because there is the physical evidence of the occurrence—the obvious V-shaped form layered along the ridge margin and flowing directly toward the crest of the MAR—it is difficult to deny that a smoking gun exists at the scene of this primordial event. This is yet another piece of evidence developing an undeniably mounting link between the period of the last ice age and the apparent rise of the MAR. It is also clear that the addition of substantial volumes of magma would have had the significant potential of raising the MAR in vertical displacements above where we find it today.

Figure 22. *The areas inside my white ovals are where the southern tip of the V formation (Reykjanes Ridge) ends and encounters the Charlie-Gibbs transform fault.Here it is clear that the magma thickened the seafloor crust (Minia Seamount) before pushing laterally toward the east, where it appears to consolidate again in irregular crustal thickening (Hecate Seamount) before gaining access to the main crest axis and then the Azores Plateau. Image by NOAA/Google.*

The force behind the migrating magma would most likely have been directed not only to pushing up the magma but also into pushing the oceanic crust upward to relieve the enormous pressure behind it.

As evidenced by the bathymetric maps of the area, initially the plume appears to have squirted out very close to the Icelandic island, but successively and over time, as the accumulating crust thickened and was caused to subside as a result of that accretion, it moved down the ridge crest. This created the V formation. This is the very effect that Vink et al. (1985) proposed.

The migrating Icelandic magma plume appears to have been following the crest of the MAR for as far along as the Azores Plateau, raising it higher and higher relative to Iceland. Meanwhile, Iceland itself was successively being pushed down by the ever-growing weight of the glaciers. So, we had two effects at once: the lowering of Iceland and the rising of the MAR near the Azores Plateau. A sort of seesaw effect was created between the two plateaus, creating an elevated gradient southward.

To complicate matters, the Icelandic hot spot plume was not directed down the crest of the MAR in a steady stream, but at any given moment in time, there could have been a new pulse of additional magma added to the flow to further pressurize it and push it past obstacles.

It is of interest to note that the Azores Plateau is that point on the MAR known as the triple plate junction. It was and still is the highest point along the ridge crest, so it's not surprising that that's where the migrating magma would have wound up—under the oceanic crust, raising the plateau still higher than it is today.

The triple plate junction is a more complicated version of the spreading center, which is represented by most of the MAR. Whereas the majority of it is the junction of two plates that are being pushed apart by the upwelling of convection currents from deep within the earth's mantle, the triple junction is a point where three plate boundaries are experiencing the lifting and separation force of convection currents that are driving the three plate segments apart. In this case, the plates involved are the North American plate, the European plate, and the African plate.

How much of a difference this will make when extra magma is added to the upwelling can be described by the same principle as the paper and slit demonstration. The slit in the paper makes it much easier for your finger to push through it. Cutting three intersecting slits dramatically reduces the structural integrity of the paper. It now becomes very easy to push the flaps open. In the case of the crust, it raises the crustal "flaps" to a higher elevation. This condition is yet another reason why the MAR around the

Azores Plateau has the potential to have risen high above sea level. Next, we need to examine what occurred when the Icelandic hot spot plume was diverted down toward the Azores Plateau.

It is a fact that during the last ice age, Iceland was capped with glaciers. Furthermore, there is clear evidence that it unquestionably caused vast quantities of magma to be squeezed down toward and under the adjacent MAR. The new infusion to the MAR would inevitably have caused that segment of the ridge, which was already substantially higher than the rest of the Atlantic basin, to rise farther still. These simultaneous processes were amplifying the uplift, which appears to have been ongoing at precisely the time frame that Plato claims Atlantis existed and subsequently sank. The evidence here appears to be gaining more momentum in favor of Plato's claims than one might have initially thought without knowing about these contemporary geologic events.

Another point to consider is that by adding the enormous volume of magma from the hot spot plume, there would have been a greater rebound effect than would ever have been predicted from isostasy alone. This effect would have been much more accentuated than what would've been produced from a rebound caused by lowered sea levels alone—but this appears to be precisely what happened. It seems that geologists do not factor in these events when they dismiss the assertions raised that Atlantis could have existed in the Atlantic Ocean.

This is all qualitative reckoning, based on what one would expect to happen if one were to consider the convergence of all these natural phenomena. But to what extent the MAR would rise would be yet another question. Would it be driven upward high enough to create a large island, one big enough to satisfy the claims made by Plato? My approach was to create an analytic process using what is known, with what is inferred, to create realistic, measurable comparisons.

The task at hand was to produce some actual numerical values for estimating the degree to which the forces unleashed at the end of the ice age contributed to the extraordinary rise of the MAR, enough to create a large island. To do so, we needed to be able to calculate how much the combination of the lowering of Iceland and the rising of the Azores Plateau would eventually uplift the MAR and whether it would be enough to satisfy the Atlantis myth and create the island Plato claimed. The next chapter explores these issues.

CHAPTER 7
CALCULATING THE RISE

This chapter will continue with a wholly qualitative discussion of how much the MAR could have risen, but I'm going to leave out the math involved. The supporting math can be found in the appendix at the end of the book. Although the math is not very complicated, (back-of-the-envelope estimates) as many know, sometimes the simplest math problems can seem daunting if we haven't brushed up on our basics for a while. I don't want the math to distract from the fundamental concept around which the book is based.

For those who need to know the how-I-got-there calculations, you can head to the appendix after reading this chapter.

As we learned in the previous chapter, the glaciers covering Iceland in the last ice age suppressed the hot spot magma plume under the island and caused it to flow toward the MAR. In trying to gauge the amount of additional uplift to the MAR caused by the migration of the plume, it seems reasonable that it should have been proportional in some degree to two primary factors. The amount that Iceland has subsided from the weight of the glaciers, could be treated as suggesting the glaciers as a downward force on a piston in a hydraulic system where a corresponding piston is pushed up at some other distant point. And, the volume of the migrating plume as a measure of predicted upward displacement. We see a similar effect in everyday life in the way that a pump works. Push down the handle of a pump and a cylinder is also pushed down. That causes air or water to be sent somewhere else. The same thing happened when the glaciers pushed down the rising magma from the hot spot plume under Iceland. The magma was sent someplace else. The hot rising magma—like the stuff in a lava lamp— sought an upward space to flow. As the magma was diverted the crust of Iceland was subsided. For the diverted magma plume, the highest elevation nearby now became the crest of the MAR.

It's known that Iceland subsided at least sixteen hundred feet, or five hundred meters, as a result of the weight of the glaciers.

To understand how much of the MAR would have to had raised to form the island claimed by Plato, we need to look at the bathymetric maps of the ocean in that region. A bathymetric map is a depiction of the discrete ocean depths in terms of connected looping lines denoting equal elevations that are drawn around the seascape. The line that traces out the shoreline at the edge of the sea is such a line, which we call sea level. In cartography terms, these lines are called isobars.

The bathymetric diagram in figure 23 depicts the MAR around the Azores. The minus-two-kilometer isobar outline could depict the size and shape of an Atlantis-like island, as was claimed by Plato. For the MAR to rise that far out of the water, it would have had to have had a change in elevation of at least sixty-five hundred feet, or about two kilometers.

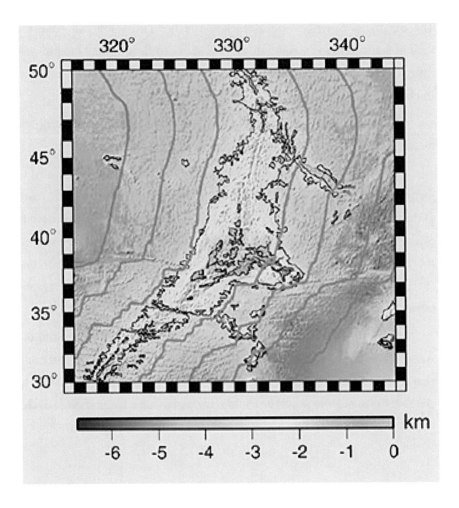

Figure 23. Bathymetric map of a section of the MAR revealing an outline, in isobars, of the shape of what could be a large island twenty-five hundred meters below sea level, according to Einar Ragnar Sigurðsson (2013). This illustrates approximately how much rise would be needed to get above sea level.

If the MAR were to rise as much as sixty-five hundred feet from below sea level around the Azores Plateau, it would produce an island larger in area than Iceland: approximately six or seven times larger in area as the central plain of Iceland that was subsided by the ice pack. Plato claimed that Atlantis was as large as Libya and Asia put together; however, we must recognize that the world was not thought of then as we know it today but rather as it is depicted in the map according to Herodotus (see figure 24). So, by today's nomenclature, Plato was talking about the land stretching roughly from the middle of North Africa to the whole of the Middle East. It is interesting to note that the map made by Herodotus makes no mention of North America as it attempts to depict the *whole* known world, but a world Plato seemed to understand differently because of his knowledge of Atlantis.

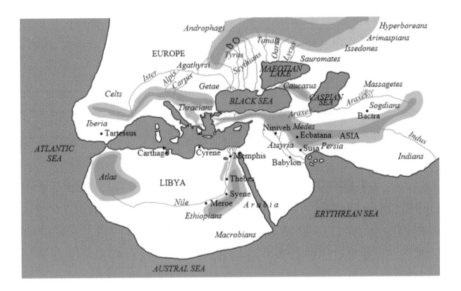

Figure 24. *Map of the world according to Herodotus (died: c. 425 BC), showing Libya and Asia as they were considered to be in ancient times. In particular, this was the way they may have appeared to Plato (GreekReporter.com).*

As we learned in earlier chapters, Plato suggested that there was a continent beyond Atlantis that surrounded the Atlantic Ocean; clearly, he was among the few who knew this.

It is easy to appreciate, then, that the ancients' understanding of the actual size of things was not accurate by today's standards. It wasn't until a

Spanish cartographer, Juan de la Cosa—who had made four voyages to the new world, including one with Columbus in the late 1400s—drew the first map showing the Americas in 1500.

The Herodotus map is obviously distorted compared to the real shape of the continents, so it's hard to say exactly how Plato perceived the actual extent of the mythical land he was attempting to portray in his Atlantis dialogues. He couldn't have believed that Atlantis was as large as the extent of Libya and Asia combined as we know them today, and we can't be sure exactly how Plato envisioned its actual size.

We must settle on a size that fits a logical calculation and is historically defensible. The calculation of the size of the island that would satisfy Plato's description has to be based on the geography that was known in that day. Judging by the Herodotus map, which is the only tangible evidence to go on, it appears that the island's largest dimension is approximately fifteen hundred miles, or about twenty-four hundred kilometers. The reason I'm concerned with only one dimension of the island will be made clear shortly.

I've already concluded that some of the misunderstanding on Plato's part about the overall extent of Atlantis comes from the way someone might approach it by sailing west from the coast of the Iberian Peninsula toward an island formed from the raised MAR. As I've said previously, when approaching the island from the east, one would encounter what would appear to be a vast island and island chain running north to south. Although the MAR might not have had as much area in square miles of land as North Africa and the Asian part of the Middle East, it would *appear* to be comparable from a north-to-south perspective as one sailed toward it and up and down its coastline.

The Azores Plateau has been elevated substantially above the rest of the surrounding MAR for some time—at least 8.12 million years (Jean-Baptiste et al. 2009; Quartau 2007)—as part of the triple plate junction, where the North American plate, Eurasian plate, and African plate's edges converge. Also, this triple junction is the location of a hot spot, like that which is under Iceland and Hawaii, but not quite so robust; there are some geologists (e.g., Sigurðsson 2013) who believe it to be active today. But there really isn't such a thing as a passive hot spot, which is sometimes referred to as a mantle plume. By their nature, they're dynamos of magmatic activity that dwarf any manmade activities. It is interesting to note once again that the place Plato chose to "locate" his Atlantis tale is one of the most dynamic parts of the earth's crust.

The mathematical challenge to predicting the amount the MAR could have risen was in analyzing and calculating the unbalancing forces created by the lowered sea levels and the displaced hot spot magma from Iceland. In other words, we needed to model the unique potential for crustal uplift around the MAR.

With a model, we're able to examine the relationship between the different variables. That will allow for the prediction of the uplifting of the rocky crust (or the sinking of it), which partly depends on how it bends under a given force.

In order to simplify the process, geologists consider the crust of the earth in terms of homogeneous slabs of bendable rock, which enables them to calculate the degree that it has subsided or rebounded from the presence of glaciers or seawater. They have good data for such places as the European continent and the Icelandic island plateau.

This approach reminds me of the calculations I've done in the past in the field of materials sciences to evaluate the bending strength of aerospace structural components and concrete support beams to determine a breaking point.

Because geologists already consider the crust of the earth in terms of the simple bending of slabs or beams, I can begin to show how a beam model might work as well as some of the surprising aspects it reveals.

For the sake of simplicity, it's fair to visualize the Icelandic crust as a big circular slab. In figure 25, the arrow simulates the force of the glaciers lying atop the crust of the island, pushing it down in the central plain and creating a saucer-shaped depression.

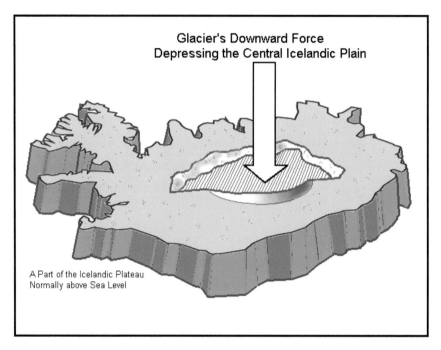

Figure 25. Schematic view of the Icelandic crust pushed into a bowl shape from the weight of the Pleistocene glaciers. Note how the crust is connected all around to other crust structures, unlike the MAR, which is unconnected in the middle (at the spreading center).

Although the glaciers covered large portions of Iceland during the Pleistocene, the extent of coverage varied according to location (see figure 26). Another variable is that the glaciers varied in thickness around the island (thickness data is not included in figure 26). The greatest buildup of glaciers was around the Vatnajökull volcano—even today it is three thousand feet thick. The data available to me (see figure 27) showed the distribution of the ice pack thickness of glaciers across the island during the Pleistocene. Judging by the current distribution of glacial ice, it's clear that the 1,625-foot subsistence (and according to Sigmundsson 2006) was in the central plain of Iceland, where the thickest ice packs exist today.

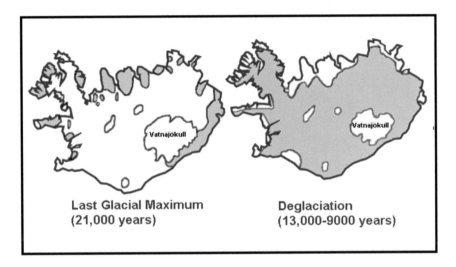

Figure 26. *Glacial ice packs on Iceland at the height of the ice age and then as the glaciers receded (Einarsson and Ingolfsson).*

The central plain is an area that includes the Vatnajökull volcano. The Vatnajökull volcano was and still is the focus of the hot spot plume that drives a major aspect of the geologic activity in Iceland. The other source of geologic activity comes from the convection cell of the spreading center that is renting Iceland. The Vatnajökull volcano sits atop the focus of the immense magma plume under Iceland and represents the identifiable and discrete force in which we are interested. This is the force that I contend was transferred down the MAR to the adjoining Azores Plateau and that lifted a large mid-Atlantic island above sea level.

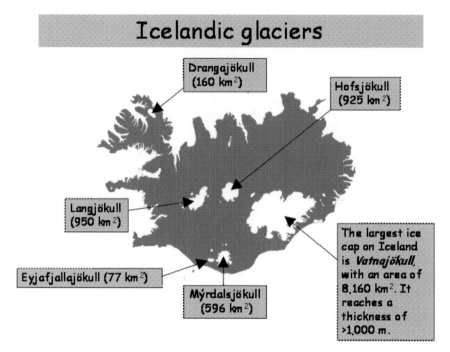

Figure 27. The distribution of glaciers across Iceland today. This diagram indicates that the most intense glacial buildup is concentrated in the six regions depicted.

I was first faced with the confounding effects of the force of the spreading center under Iceland on the subsidence and rebound of the central plain of Iceland. How the spreading center influenced the rebound dynamics and how to separate it out from the rising magma of the hot spot was at first a problem. But I came to recognize that the spreading center was a relative constant. The subsidence of the plain was a result of the glaciers pushing down against both forces—the hot spot and the spreading center. When the hot spot was diverted away from the center of Iceland, the spreading center of magma remained a constant upward pressure. So, the rebound recorded was only attributable to the return of the hot spot plume.

I considered the amount that the Azores Plateau was raised by the redirection of the hot spot plume as a function of its redistribution over the larger area at the MAR and specifically, the Azores Plateau.

Figure 27 depicts the general extent of the glacial distribution across the island. According to Ólafur Ingólfsson (n.d.), professor of glacial and quaternary geology in the University of Iceland's Department of Geology and Geography and Institute of Earth Sciences, 11 percent of the island is currently covered with glaciers. Much more of the island was covered during the Pleistocene, but we know that the area of glaciation that depressed the crust 1,625 feet was not the total area of the island.

In examining figure 27, we can conservatively say that at least half of the island was covered with glaciers thick enough to contribute to the subsidence. That would be about twenty thousand square miles. This is an important number to keep in mind as we go forward with our process. Because the island of Atlantis must be larger than Iceland by definition (i.e. Plato), the force of the displaced hot spot magma will be spread out over a larger area. The force per unit area will be less as a result. Therefore, the forces of the displaced magma on the MAR and the Azores Plateau will have been diluted by a factor of the difference in geographical area between them - considering the twenty-thousand-square-mile Iceland zone.

Figure 28 depicts two types of crustal slabs. The thick simple beam shows the effort of rebound uplift on the thick crust of the Icelandic Plateau. The thin cantilevered beam represents the effort of rebound or uplift on the thin crust of the MAR with the same amount of force. The up-and-down flexibility of a slab of crust is the same in each direction.

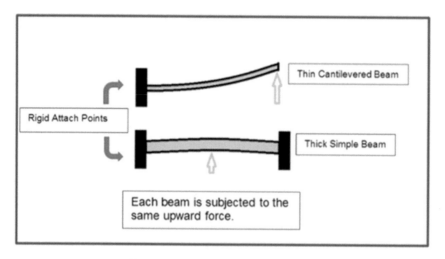

Figure 28. Illustration of how the same force produces different magnitudes of upward deflection.

The amount of force to push down the Icelandic crust is equal to the force to return it to the opposite uplifted position. The same holds true for any section of crust, and that includes the crust of the MAR.

If we take the same force that the glaciers impart downwardly on the Icelandic crust and now apply it to uplifting the crust of the MAR, we can immediately see that that force is going to have a much greater effect on the thin crust of the MAR. It's once again the analogy of a thick diving board being harder to deflect downwardly than it would for a thinner one. But the MAR crust is not only thinner but also a divided, spreading center crust.

Now we can see that the analogy of the paper with a slit cut into it is appropriate as it responds in different ways to an upward or downward force compared to the paper without a slit. The response to force of the thin-crust MAR is amplified compared to what it was on the thicker Icelandic crust. If the glaciers forced the Icelandic crust down sixteen hundred feet, we should expect the same force to raise the thin crust of the MAR a measurable amount more than sixteen hundred feet.

Figure 29 depicts the cross section of the oceanic crust around the MAR. It demonstrates a different structure from the inland continental crusts – in this case the crust of the Icelandic Plateau. Inasmuch as the MAR has articulated crust at its central edge, it permits a more exaggerated response to forces either loading it or trying to uplift it.

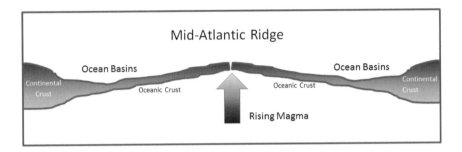

Figure 29. *Diagram depicting the cross section of the MAR, the ocean basins, and the connecting continental crusts. At the center is the rising magma plume that adds additional elevation to the MAR.*

Normally, the crust of the MAR is considerably more elevated than the rest of the Atlantic seafloor because of the powerful upwelling of magmatic convection cells that cause the opposing continental crusts to spread in opposite directions—the so-called continental drift. So, it's clear that the crust of the MAR is not firmly connected at its inner margins. If we want to compare how the same forces act on different parts of the crust, we must treat each crust variant differently. The crust of the Icelandic Plateau is clearly different from that of the mid-ocean ridges, and we can't expect them to react the same way to those similar forces.

The crust of the MAR is not only different from the crust of Iceland because of its difference in thickness but also in its structure. Also, the MAR at the Azores Plateau consists of not just one spreading center seam but of three seams, or faults, in its crust. It is a triple plate junction, so it should be expected to react even more dramatically than just a simple two-plate spreading center might.

The Icelandic crust, on the other hand, is also above a spreading center, but that spreading activity is buried much more deeply into the lithosphere, than that of the oceanic counterpart. Occasionally, the magmatic activity reaches the surface, but by and large, its energies are more directed to distorting the crust of the island and to creating the overall spreading phenomena. The ability of the Icelandic crust to flex like a diving board is marginal and very limited compared to the much thinner oceanic crust.

How the differences in the structure of these crusts bear on the way they react to the forces that rise beneath will reveal how they will produce significantly different magnitudes of reaction in the form of uplift and subsistence.

Recall that the two different crusts that we are examining are the cantilevered beam (one end attached) and the simple beam (attached at both ends). My examination of the tables of beam deflection calculations posted by Iowa State University's Department of Engineering (appearing in the appendix) reveals that a cantilevered beam could have sixteen times the deflection to an applied force than a simple beam. The cantilevered beam represents the oceanic crust and the simple beam represents the crust associated with the Icelandic Plateau. In other words, the same force will have different effects on different kinds of the earth's crusts. Not surprisingly, a given force will affect a thin crust more dramatically than it will a thick crust.

When the magma plume from the hot spot was able to resume rising under Iceland, it lifted the plateau crust by over sixteen hundred feet. That is nearly the same amount of magma that invariably had to have migrated down the crest of the MAR to the Azores Plateau. There, on the thinner crust, that same magma plume would have had a considerably greater impact toward raising the plateau per unit area—very much more than it had on the Icelandic Plateau.

So, it's easy to understand this concept—thin crust bends more easily than thick crust, and crust restrained at only one end is much more flexible than crust that is completely restrained. But there are more effects at play that must be accounted for to develop a qualitative estimate of how much the MAR could rise. This is important because to completely make the case for Plato's claim, it must be shown that the MAR, and the Azores Plateau, could rise high enough to make a substantial island. Plato was emphatic that the island of Atlantis was substantial—as large as those of his time believed the distance from Libya to Asia was.

We've learned that when the magma plume from the Icelandic hot spot was diverted down the crest of the MAR, it traveled toward the Azores Plateau. If the island that it theoretically helped to create was as big as Plato claimed, then it would have been larger than the Icelandic Plateau because in no way would anyone confuse Iceland with an area as large as a part of Libya plus the Levant. But it is obvious that the force arriving at the Azores Plateau would have been dissipated over this larger area. The area that would be comparable to Plato's understanding of geography would be about six or seven times the area of the Icelandic Plateau. This leads us to assume that the magma force would have been dissipated by the difference in the areas.

To begin getting to the dynamic uplift we are seeking, we must use the factor of how easily the MAR crust bends compared to that of the thick crust of the Icelandic Plateau.

The bendability of the crust is dependent on several factors that scientists refer to as flexural rigidity, as discussed earlier. For our application, flexural rigidity can be boiled down to merely a matter of the thickness of the crust. In my role as an aerospace materials scientist, I used flexural rigidity sensors to monitor the flexing of aircraft and spacecraft structures as they were experimentally tested.

Before a new type of aircraft is put into service, the wings and cabin of a test article are subjected to extreme conditions in which repetitive cycles of flexing are induced to determine the point at which the structure will fail. The cabins are inflated and deflated until cracks appear in the rivet holes. The wings are bent up and down, like you'd bend a paper clip, until cracks form.

For any aircraft, each takeoff and landing flexes the cabin wings and landing gear. Airliners are pressurized to maintain passenger comfort, and with every flight, they are subjected to the cabin being slightly inflated and deflated according to the outside atmospheric pressures. High altitudes, with the associated low outside pressures, cause the aircraft to slightly inflate. Returning to the ground, the aircraft cabin is slightly deflated as the outside air pressure increases and balances things out. These cycles create cracks in the aircraft structure. This phenomenon is known as fatigue. It causes cracks in materials besides paper clips. This was what I was concerned with in my aerospace studies. To measure the degree of mechanical flexure, I used flexural rigidity sensors. But here with the earth's crust, we're not so concerned about the nature of materials cracking than we are with their ability to bend and, more importantly, with the contrast of flexibility of the earth's crust as it is found in different places.

Getting back to the issue of the contrast of the degree that one type of crust will flex versus another, the common factor reduces to the thickness of the material being bent. After all, in the discussion of flexural rigidity and fatiguing paper clips, we find once again that the issue really boils down to a simple and easily understandable concept—it's easier to bend something that is thin as opposed to the same material that is thick.

In the case of the Icelandic versus the MAR crust, this is exactly what we are concerned with—thick versus thin. There are formulae that enable one to calculate these flexibility differences as the thickness varies.

Now we have four phenomena to consider in calculating the amount of the supposed MAR and Azores Plateau rise: the isostatic rebound, the crust flexibility by thickness, whether the crust is cantilevered, and how dissipated the magma became while filling an area several times larger than Iceland.

It was shown that the issue of how the crusts are attached to adjacent land structures is yet another factor to consider. We dealt with that in terms of cantilevered and simple beam bending. In that exercise, we saw that the cantilevered beam would be sixteen times as springy as the simple beam model – that is, the MAR versus Iceland.

Furthermore, we discussed the issue of how the thickness of the crust bears on flexibility in the consideration of flexural rigidity. That examination revealed that doubling the thickness had enormous effects on the flexibility of the crust. As an example, if we take two rock slabs, one that is one kilometer thick and another that is two kilometers thick, the same force applied to both would give the one-kilometer-thick slab eight times the deflection as that same force applied to the two-kilometer-thick slab! This means that doubling the thickness makes it eight times as rigid and resistant to bending.

The takeaway here is simple: a thicker beam is harder to bend than a thinner one of the same materials—but by a lot.

According to the equation that describes this phenomenon, the amount of force required to bend a beam, or plate, increases exponentially so that a thin plate would be much easier to bend than one twice as thick.

Conversely, halving the thickness causes the beam to undergo eight times the deflection, or bending. So, forces under a thin oceanic crust would cause it to be uplifted much higher than the same force under a continental crust—on a one-to-one basis, the oceanic crust should be eight times as flexible for each halving of the thickness! There is unquestionably a great difference in thickness between the crust of the MAR and that of Iceland. Mid-Atlantic crest crust around the Azores averages about fifteen kilometers thick, whereas Iceland averages twenty-nine kilometers thick, according to Allen et al. (2002). The crust of the Icelandic Plateau is at least two times as thick as the crust of the MAR. That would mean that the MAR would potentially react to a force from below with $2 \times 2 \times 2$ times the rise, or potentially eight times as much rise as the same force on the subsided Icelandic crust.

This seems to be borne out by our observation of the oceanic ridge system that girdles the world that is caused by the convection cells rising around the plate boundaries.

Let's backtrack for a moment concerning the articulation of the crust along the diverging spreading centers. I shouldn't make it seem that the oceanic spreading centers are like fully unrestrained, articulated, and cantilevered beams. I don't want to cloud the issue with this point, as we will see later, about whether the diverging slabs of crust at the spreading centers are fully unconnected or mostly unconnected. Let's just say for the sake of argument that the junction between the adjoining plates is a tenuously connected union (see figure 30), and here is the reason why. Imagine two pieces of red-hot molten metal plates touching along their edges. The point where they touch may essentially be molten but has some connecting adhesion. But that adhesion is extremely weak. According to Vishal et al. (2011), rock loses 70 percent of its tensile strength at 250°C. The rising magma is much hotter than that and raises the temperature of the edges of the crust well beyond the 250°C point. So, the edges of the plates at the spreading centers are only touching with a weakly held connection, and the rock has lost almost all its ability to resist being flexed (like a diving board) by the force of rising magma.

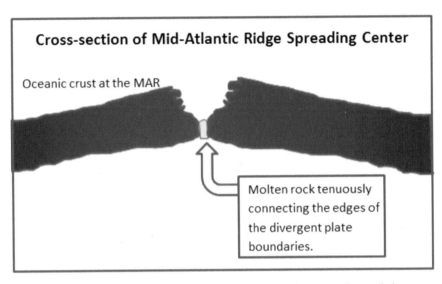

Figure 30. *Simplified close-up view of the MAR cross section showing molten rock that tenuously connects the edges of the plate boundaries.*

The concept of the cantilevered beam holds if we think of the plate edge junction as two diving boards that are facing each other and held together with molten rock that is reduced to a thick, toothpaste-like consistency. My only concern here however is that the spreading centers are submerged. Since I was unable to find studies that addressed the strength of heated rock quenched by seawater, I've reduced the amount that I calculated the percentage of weakening. To be conservative, assume that the effective springiness of the diving boards is reduced not by 70 percent but by only 50 percent. I'm going to base the weakening of that point where the crusts are in contact, as it is heated above 250°C as losing 50 percent of its tensile strength. So instead of being sixteen times the uplift that occurred to Iceland, it should be calculated as a little more than eight times as springy as that. When adding the springiness contributed by how thin the crust of the MAR is, we can also conservatively multiply that by 50 percent of the flexural rigidity. That would reduce the flexure from eight to about four (from the rigidity calculations).

Using all these known phenomena, we can now begin to reconstruct the overall process, step-by-step.

To match Plato's claim that Atlantis was equal in extent to "Libya and Asia" combined, we can see from the bathymetric map in figure 23 that the Azores Plateau would have to rise over sixty-five hundred feet, or over two thousand meters, to expose enough land to give that appearance. Now, if it can be shown that this was the degree that the plateau rose, we'll be home free!

The process begins during the last ice age, when the ocean levels dropped dramatically. With the ocean levels so much lower, the forces of isostatic compensation beneath started the process of uplifting the MAR considerably above where it was before. The isostatic rebound will raise the MAR enough that when Iceland is capped and the hot spot plume is diverted and nowhere else to go, it will see the Azores Plateau area of the MAR as the highest adjacent elevation and ascend in that direction—according to the theory developed by Vink et al. (1985).

The bathymetric map in figure 31 shows that the hypothetically exposed MAR representing Atlantis shows a large raised area that was larger in area than the capped-off area of Iceland. I'm pointing that out because the disparity in area is a factor in the amount the diverted magma will raise the MAR. The capped-off hot spot plume, diverted down the axis of the MAR, would have had a diminished effect in raising the MAR and the Azores Plateau—that is, the magma would have been spread out over this new, larger area.

From our previous calculations, the cantilevered beam model for the hot oceanic crust junction is estimated to have eight times the ability to bend upwardly than that of the Icelandic crust.

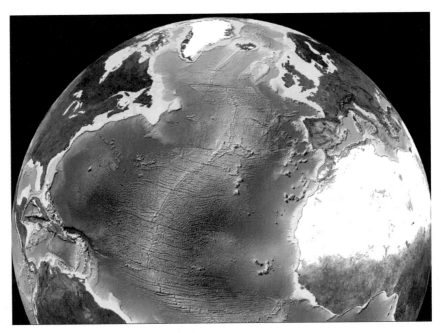

Figure 31. *Satellite relief map of the mid-Atlantic Ocean seafloor (NOAA), revealing the outline of the Azores Plateau that may be representative of the general location of the Atlantean island.*

I've traced the outline of the Atlantis island shoreline on Google Earth to determine its area (see figure 32). The area of the island would be about 141,000 square miles. I've shown that the area of the central plain of Iceland that rebounded 1,625 feet was about 20,000 square miles.

The exposed MAR could be, according to our calculations, at least six times the area of Iceland, including only the areas that were subsided in the central plain. So, in calculating the uplifting force of the Iceland diverted magma, we must divide our result by six.

If we combine all the geodynamic phenomena and characteristics we've discussed as a formula, we can make an equation that looks like this:

$R_1 + ((C_B \times F_R \times R_2)/A) = \text{Total Rise}$

Where,

R_1 = the MAR rise from lowered sea level = 1/3 the drop in sea level × 3, the amount the MAR is normally higher than average seafloor) = 420

C_B = multiplier of cantilevered crust versus simple beam crust (16 × .50 = 8)

F_R = flexural rigidity factor as a function of crust thickness 29/15 ≈ 2, 2^3 = 8, 8 × .50 = 4

R_2 = glacial rebound of Icelandic Plateau (+1,625)

A = area differential between Iceland and the MAR (1:7.1) Area disparity 141k/20k ≈ 7.1

Substituting values into the equation, we get the following:

420 feet + ((8 × 4 × 1,625)/7.1 ≈ 7,743-foot rise

The answer we get, 7,743 feet, is a little bigger than what we estimated from guessing the size of an island as big as part of North Africa to the Levant. We also used the bathymetric chart to refine the size and shape according to how much the MAR would have to rise to get the size island we were estimating. So, it turns out that we are really very close to our estimate.

The rise I'm proposing seems improbable, but when we consider the enormous forces at play beneath the MAR and the nearby Azores Plateau—the spreading center plume, the split crust in the seafloor from the spreading center, the seafloor isostasy from the lowered sea level, the migrated Icelandic hot spot plume, and the remnants of the hot spot under the Azores Plateau—it becomes clear that perhaps these numbers are not so unrealistic, afterall.

Because the area around the Azores is already above sea level, the MAR would be at least four thousand feet above sea level and higher at the interior of the island. Some mountains would have been even higher, since the Azores are themselves well above sea level. We should also take into consideration that Mount Pico on the Azores is seventy-seven hundred feet above sea level today. I could add in other phenomena to increase the height above sea level that the MAR could reach, but I think enough has been said, and I don't want to complicate this any more than it is already. I think I've made my point.

I've shown that the Azores Plateau could have risen several thousand feet above sea level, enough to easily reach the two-thousand-meter isobars on the bathymetric map—to reveal enough landmass to produce a large island off the coast of Spain at the time and place that Plato claimed! (See figures 32 and 33.)

A more detailed mathematical proof of this hypothesis would be necessary to gain a more accurate result. Further investigation with the use of more powerful computational simulations is not within the scope of this book. But it is believed that the representation of these beam bending and flexural rigidity models hold up as well as the Middleton/Wilcock models currently in use to make quick, simplified calculations that produce useful, rough order-of-magnitude results.

Before continuing, I'd like to add that, presently, geologists are on an accelerated learning curve for understanding the geology of the earth and tectonic activity. Yet geologists can't accurately predict earthquakes or volcanic eruptions or the tsunamis they generate. And as we know from computer simulations of weather, in particular about hurricanes, there may be significant differences in the predictions and results from one computer model to the next, as we saw when Hurricane Sandy veered toward America's East Coast in 2012. One National Oceanic and Atmospheric Administration computer simulation had Sandy veering out to sea, while another had it running along the coast. Yet completely at odds, a European computer model had Sandy veering directly into the coast around New York City, which turned out to be the case.

In the field of geology, there are several competing geophysical theories and corresponding simulations concerning the morphology, rheology (the study of magma flow), and dynamics operating within the earth's mantle, representing the layers beneath the earth's crust. Scientists use simulations of physical events to be able to study them in a controlled environment. What I've done is to conduct my own simulation in a simple sense by using the gedankenexperiments—the mind experiments that Albert Einstein initially used to formulate the basic aspects of his theory of relativity—then make best-fit, order-of-magnitude calculations. So, to address anyone's concerns, the facts and calculations that I've laid out in this chapter are as good as it gets.

We've shown that a large island could have existed at the time and place Plato claimed, but what about where it went? Obviously, it's not there today, which leads to the question of what caused it to sink, as Plato claimed. This certainly is the most well-known aspect of the Atlantean story and the most exciting part of all the fictional movies and books about it. I'm not sure if I'm obligated to show that phase of the Atlantis myth, but fortunately I can! The next chapter will explain what happened to the mysterious mythical island that existed so long ago, when mammoths, saber-toothed tigers, and other ice age animals were roaming the earth and humans were painting their images on cave walls.

Figure 32. *Bathymetric measurements of the MAR using seventy-two-hundred-foot-depth gradient lines to reveal my outline (in white) of Atlantis toward the end of the last ice age. North Africa appears to the right, with the tip of the Iberian Peninsula to the upper right and Iceland and Greenland in the upper-left corner. These other coastlines do not reflect lowered sea levels.*

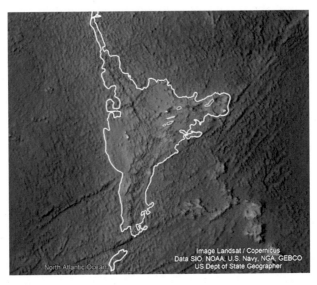

Figure 33. *A closer look at my outline of Atlantis superimposed on the NOAA survey map with the present-day Azores islands appearing in the eastern region.*

CHAPTER 8
ATLANTIS: SINKING TO OBLIVION

Now you can appreciate why I am certain that a large island once existed in the mid-Atlantic Ocean just before the end of the last ice age. But that island is obviously gone. If it did exist, where is it today? So many detractors of the claims in Plato's dialogues about Atlantis ask, "How could such a gigantic island have existed once and now have vanished? It fails all respectable logic." But I've laid out what I believe is convincing evidence that demonstrates how this island evolved; now I will demonstrate why it is not around today.

The story of Atlantis wouldn't be complete unless I was able to explain the dramatic sinking in its totality; how it suddenly sank is almost as important as how it appeared. Therefore, an explanation of that defining and apocalyptic event is in order. Did it sink as precipitously as Plato claimed, and if so, how and why?

Was the sinking of that great Atlantic island a foregone conclusion, the consequence of something we can explain? Can we use what we've learned from the raising of the MAR to explain why it sank, and if so, can we explain how or why it sank with relative swiftness, as implied by Plato?

The answer to the inevitability of its rising and the swiftness of its disappearance is a resounding yes. But if we merely run the clock backward, we might not readily see how it would be possible; for one thing, everything involving the glaciers is a slow and grinding process, involving many thousands, even millions, of years. Plato implied, on the other hand, that Atlantis sank with some rapidity, and many claim that he meant it happened in a night and a day. In fact, I believe that notion is a misinterpretation of Plato's dialogues. It is, however, easy to see how one might interpret Plato's words that way:

> *But afterwards [subsequent to a major battle] there occurred violent earthquakes and floods; and in a single day and night of misfortune all your warlike men in a body sank into the earth, and the island of Atlantis in like manner disappeared in the depths of the sea.*

This passage is the one that has evidently created the image of Atlantis sinking overnight from "violent earthquakes and floods." It is understandable why anyone would have the impression that the demise of Atlantis was sudden.

First, I should say that earthquakes are still not uncommon in the Mediterranean basin; because of plate tectonics, the African plate is moving north and colliding with the European plate. This plate tectonic motion is what has produced iconic mountain peaks such as the Matterhorn. So, Plato and his contemporaries were aware that these geological events occurred, and cataclysm is always a grand backdrop for drama. This would surely be a great plot device to hold an audience's attention and to make the story appear more dramatically realistic.

But we should take into consideration some other interpretations of what he said. There are two parts that talk about two different things but that are connected with the words "like manner." "Like manner" doesn't mean to do something in exactly the same way but in a similar one. "They fought like cats and dogs" doesn't mean two people literally fought by scratching and biting each other. According to my hypothesis and calculations, I interpret what Plato is saying in another way. I believe he means to say that the whole of Atlantis sank into the ocean in the way that "warlike men in a body" sink into the earth—not necessarily in one day and night, just that Atlantis sank or disappeared.

I make that distinction because it is difficult to form a rational argument that an island as large as Plato claimed Atlantis to be was able to sink that rapidly. The rest of his story concerning the size, shape, and location of the island can be accommodated geologically, but that it sank so quickly is much more difficult to justify. However, I believe that Plato's statement about how quickly Atlantis sank is ambiguous and could easily be interpreted otherwise than that it sank in a day and a night. Because everything else seems to fit, I'm hedging on the fact that he meant "in like manner" to refer to the whole island sinking as one piece, or as a body.

Now, as I've discovered in my research, it probably did mean that it sank quite rapidly by geological measures, though not in a day and a night. This leads to another interpretation: Plato believed that Atlantis sank with great rapidity because that was how the Sais priests conveyed the legend to Solon, thus compelling him to believe in its fast demise, but we should apply geological terms when we think of it happening quickly or overnight.

Plato later says:

And the island of Atlantis in like manner disappeared in the depths of the sea. For which reason the sea in those parts is impassable and impenetrable, because there is a shoal of mud in the way; and this was caused by the subsidence of the island.

Once again, I'm going to show, by employing some logical and scientifically based reasoning, that we can come to an understanding of how that all happened.

We can look at it both ways because it's not really clear what happened to the hypothetical island.

It's generally accepted that the advance of the glaciers stopped about twenty thousand years ago; therefore, it stands to reason that glaciers began to melt sometime around that period. Of course, we've learned that glaciers take much longer to build up than to melt away (see figure 34).

I'm reemphasizing this because I believe that it's something we should be cognizant of with regard to the global warming and sea-level rise occurring today.

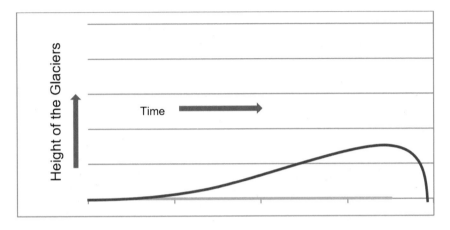

Figure 34. *Graph of the glacial buildup to the glacial melting.*

As I discussed previously, glaciers are formed by the small amount of snow that falls in high mountains and in frigid climates such as Greenland and Antarctica, the continent that, surprisingly, has one of the lowest rates of precipitation on earth. One aspect of cold climates is that when the temperature gets very cold—in Antarctica, very, very cold—moisture is squeezed out of the air, leaving very little for precipitation, such as snow. What follows is that the little snow that does fall can make it through the summer months, which is easy in Antarctica, and it becomes yet another incremental layer of a glacier. On and on the glacier slowly builds, and because the air is so dry with little precipitation, the process takes a very long time. The Pleistocene glaciers began building about two million years ago and finally stopped twenty thousand years ago. From twenty thousand years ago until eleven thousand years ago, the melting of the glaciers was well on its way, and that's only about ten thousand years to undo what it took two million to do! By this metric, the glaciers melted two hundred times faster than they built up. The point I'm trying to make here is that the relatively rapid meltdown had its consequences.

As the glaciers melted, the water poured back into the oceans, and they began to rise. The rise was much quicker than the lowering simply because the melting process was much faster than the process of glacial buildup. There had to have been a complete reversal of the effects we discussed earlier: the increasing weight of the rising sea levels caused the MAR to become inundated and pushed down. The higher the sea level rose, the more dramatic the subsiding effect.

But simultaneously, there was another factor occurring with regard to the mythical island. The glaciers were not only melting in North America, Europe, and Asia but also in Iceland. It's easy to imagine what had to have happened next. The melting of the glaciers in Iceland released the cap on the hot spot, allowing the Icelandic Plateau to rise. The magma needn't go anywhere else now; it could go back to pumping straight up under Iceland. Iceland rose and is still rising, but the bottom line is that the island of Atlantis would then have had to sink. All the things holding it up were removed as the glaciers melted and rising sea levels adding weight. There was no other alternative.

Now let's think about how fast it sank. There is no question that it would have to sink, and it could have done so over a shorter period than it took to rise, which was the entire time the glaciers were forming over the Northern Hemisphere: about 190,000 years. As the glaciers melted—which was, remember, about twenty thousand years ago—Atlantis would have begun the process of sinking. So, it seems that there would have been a slow part of the subsistence at first, but we don't know if there would have been a sudden end.

If we go back to the point Plato makes about there being hot springs under a large extent of the island of Atlantis, that may be a clue to its final but sudden demise. The part of the MAR that is still above sea level is the Azores, and there are hot springs there. There was also an abundance of hot springs in Iceland before the glaciation, as there are today. It would be logical to think that, with the added magma from the Icelandic plume, there would be ample components for abundant hot springs on Atlantis. If we consider the oceanic crust being thinner than the crust of the continents and Iceland—in general five kilometers versus forty kilometers— then any rebound resulting from the melting of the glaciers may very well have been accentuated by the thin oceanic crust. Instead of the slow process of rebound we observe as the thick continental crust subsides, we may have seen the converse: a rapid rise and disastrously rapid sinking of the MAR's seafloor.

The hot springs still evident today in the Azores and mentioned in Plato's description of Atlantis are dead giveaways to the magmatic activity below the MAR. We've learned that the MAR is only part of the belt of ocean spreading centers that encircle the earth and have many geological aspects in common.

The Pacific Ocean has a corresponding spreading center called the East Pacific Rise (EPR), which shows the same distinct elevation disparity to the adjoining seafloor as well as the faulting we observe at the MAR (Macdonald and Luyendyk 1981). Furthermore, since the EPR is a spreading center, it shares other similarities with the MAR. Beneath the EPR is a convection current that flows up from below the mantle—the same as the MAR. There is also a mountain range associated with it. According to the study by Macdonald and Luyendyk, a magma chamber exists that sits above the rising convection plume, just below the seafloor crust that they refer to as a cupola. Further study by Hékinian (1984) discovered that the cupola had become a huge hollowed-out chamber beneath the seafloor. It was also realized that large quantities of steam and magma can accumulate in these chambers without an immediate access for escaping.

In the areas of the EPR studied, it was noted that after a lava-flow drains from the cupola, a thin roof is formed that is supported by vent pillars (hollow tubes of cooled lava that conveyed magma to the surface) left over from the waning stages of the upwelling of the convection plume. Over time, the roof collapsed.

I found it intriguing that the MAR appears to have these formations all along its crest. In fact, a rift valley runs continuously along the crest of the MAR, suspiciously mimicking the profile of the EPR. Although it is believed that the rift valley has other mechanisms for its creation, part of that process may very well have been the cupola formation-and-collapse scenario.

It doesn't seem unreasonable to imagine that larger chambers than the EPR may have at one time formed under the MAR, since the magma upwelling and lava flows there are considerably greater. I'm afraid that I'm going to be attacked by the geologists for this speculation, but I haven't found any reason in my research that it couldn't have merit. Some might argue that in Iceland the spreading center is evident as canyons in the landscape, but and an explanation for that could be they are created above sea level and form without the cupola effect.

However, if some of the oceanic rift valleys were at one time associated with magma chambers when the migrating Icelandic magma stopped flowing, it may also have been possible that they formed similar structures to the EPR, with its hollow chambers and thin roof that eventually became at risk of collapse. If those hollow chambers had formed, they would have become a place for steam to accumulate, such as occurs in Yosemite, and the thin roof may have eventually collapsed. We know what happened to Mount Saint Helens when the earthquakes preceding the major eruption caused the huge landslide that uncorked the building pressure and explosively released the hot gas in the magma as the steam formed beneath it. So, I'm going to speculate that that phenomenon may also have contributed to the demise of the Atlantis island – if in nothing more than a horrendous human cataclysm in the late stages of sinking as the ground suddenly collapsed over an area of many hundred square miles up and down the MAR.

It seems that the sinking may have followed this pattern:

- The last ice age gradually comes to an end with the recession of the glaciers.

- The glacier's gradual buildup is reversed by rapid melting.

- Rapid glacier melting refills and raises the ocean levels at a higher rate than the process of lowering.

- The increasing weight of the rising oceans reverses the isostatic forces on the MAR—the MAR begins to subside.

- The pressure of the glaciers on the Icelandic hot spot is removed by their melting.

- The plume's path-of-least-resistance gradient from the Icelandic hot spot to the MAR is reversed.

- The magma of the hot spot plume resumes flowing up under the Icelandic island.

- The MAR loses the magma plume and settles back beneath the waves.

But along the way, some things contributed to quicken the subsidence of the MAR that I believe would have contributed to that acceleration.

When the MAR is submerged, the blanketing effect of water has the ability to remove heat from solids (such as rock) at a very high rate, at a higher rate than most other substances, especially gases such as air. When submerged, the heat of the convection plume beneath could be absorbed at a rate that was much greater than the rate it could be absorbed if the MAR were exposed to only the air above sea level. The result would be that while underwater, the MAR would lose its heat to the seawater at a higher rate than to the open air. When things are heated, they expand. When the MAR rose above sea level, the heat acquired from the convection plume would not be dissipated as rapidly as it would when submerged, so the net effect is that the MAR would have incrementally expanded as it rose. It would have attained a slightly increased volume than when submerged. When this process was reversed at the end of the ice age, the MAR would have not only begun to submerge but also to be reduced in volume. The combined result is that the MAR would have appeared to more rapidly sink, since, as it sank, the water would have absorbed the heat faster—heat previously contributing to volumetric expansion—than it would have if it had not expanded at all.

Furthermore, the expansion would have stressed the crust of the MAR and created an expansive network of fractures and faults. We all know what happens around fault lines.

Because the glaciers melted much more quickly than they formed, the ice capping the Icelandic Plateau would have also melted more quickly than it formed and more quickly provided a way for the hot spot plume to work its way back to its original path under the plateau. As the Icelandic Plateau rebounded from isostatic compensation and the return of the hot spot plume, the MAR would have more rapidly lost the necessary magma support to maintain its position above sea level, and it began to sink. The sinking would have been much faster than the rising and would have put stress on the MAR that it hadn't experienced with the rise. Recalling the fact that the MAR would likely be riddled with fractures and faults, its disposition to become unstable would have greatly increased.

The rapid withdrawal of magma from under the MAR may have created the same type of magma chambers that we see under the EPR. In the case of those formations, it has been shown that they eventually, but catastrophically, collapse.

It should become clear that as the ice waned, the MAR must have grown more and more unstable. The sinking would then have put the stressed crust at risk.

If, as I have speculated, huge magma chambers were running the length of the ridge, they would have become at risk of catastrophic collapse as the fragile eggshell-like chambers lost enormous volumes of magma and steam. The shrinking of the ridge created stress in the exposed areas of the crust, which was already faulted from its origins as fractured oceanic rock.

As the magma chambers inevitably and progressively collapsed, seawater gained access and contacted the magma. The ensuing eruptions would have been like a continual Krakatoa erupting repeatedly, issuing unimaginable volumes of steam and shock waves from earthquakes and landslides and thus generating a tsunami.

As we saw in April 2010, the eruption of the **volcano** in southern **Iceland's** Eyjafjallajökull glacier created an enormous ash cloud that quickly spread around Europe, eventually interrupting commercial air traffic for six days.

When the clouds of steam from the collapsing MAR volcanoes finally condensed back to water, a period of considerable rain would have undoubtedly followed. And simultaneously, the eustatic sea levels—the changes of sea level due to changes in the earth's crust such as postglacial rebound after the glaciers melted—would have risen commensurate with the dynamic changes occurring at the end of the last ice age.

It is clear that there would have been worldwide impact from such a massive geological event.

Scientists know that there was a worldwide event during this same period known as the Younger Dryas, when global temperatures dropped significantly just as the last ice age was ending and the earth was beginning to warm. The onset of the Younger Dryas was extremely rapid in geological terms, taking only decades and dropping the global temperatures by 3.6 degrees, to 10.8°C (from 58° to 51°F), according to Carlson (2013). This is an enormous temperature swing, completely reversing the previous onset of warming and throwing the earth back into a glacial climate once again. The Younger Dryas was a dramatic climatic event, yet it only lasted about thirteen hundred years, according to Björck (2013). So, as quickly as it started, its end was rapid too.

The process and events I'm suggesting could be an explanation of a rapid collapse of a large portion of the Atlantis island, enough so that, combined with the concurrent ongoing subsistence, it could have created a catastrophic end to the habitability of the island.

There were many things going on during the end of the ice age, as we now know: warming of the worldwide climate (attributed by some to the precession of the earth's axis and by some to the release of carbon dioxide, a greenhouse gas, from the southern oceans), melting of the glaciers, rising of the sea levels, rebounding of the continental and Icelandic crust, and releasing of the hot spot under Iceland, just to name a few that are well known. As we all recognize, one thing can lead to another and can often result in unforeseen consequences. Humans do it all the time—nature is no exception. The unforeseen consequences of natural events here, I believe, are the rising and then the sinking of the MAR.

In 1989 it was discovered that there was a worldwide rise in sea level occurring rapidly, in geologic terms, over a three-hundred-year span during one of the melting phases at the end of the last ice age. That rise was calculated to be between sixteen and twenty-five meters according to Fairbanks (1989). Such a rise today would be catastrophic, inundating vast areas of inhabited coastlines; countries such as Bangladesh would have nearly half of their area submerged. There are varied differences of opinion about how and why this event, commonly referred to as meltwater pulse 1A, occurred, but it did (see figure 35), and it may have had a contributing effect on the rapid demise of the island of Atlantis. I conjecture that it occurred around fourteen thousand years ago, at a time when it would have had an influence on the already initiated process that had begun by submerging the MAR beneath the rising sea levels.

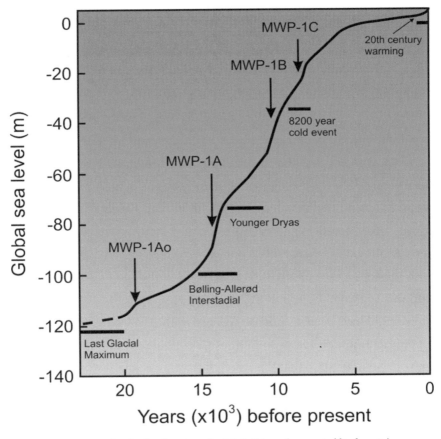

Figure 35. *Graph of meltwater pulse 1A (wikiwand.com – public domain).*

It's hard to tell whether the sinking of the island was actually a slow or quick process, but as you can see, there seems to be evidence for the latter. Gathering from what Plato says, it is hard to *prove* that the scenario of rapid sinking occurred. His words could be construed both ways. Adding to the lack of clarity, he says that the warring armies of Atlantis and the Mediterranean were stopped by some titanic geological upheaval and that the armies were swallowed up by the event. The end of the conflict, as both sides withdrew to their respective countries, could have created a period of isolation that provided the gap in time necessary for Atlantis to sink slowly, perhaps into temporary anonymity. Eventually, through who knows how long a period—decades, centuries, or eons—some may have ventured beyond the western coast of Europe to find the muddy shoals that Plato says were the only remains of the once-proud island kingdom of Atlantis.

Nevertheless, evidence remains that the MAR must have risen above sea level only to be once again submerged. The end of Atlantis, whether coming by a swift blow or several stages over time, was a catastrophic event either way.

So, it seems that the theory I'm presenting on its face could have been predicted by the geological community by now if the topic of Atlantis wasn't so taboo… comparable to UFOs. There is an answer to the question of why this theoretical approach has escaped every reputable scientist. I suppose the answer is that this is not an obvious thing and that it is tainted with the appearance of scientific quackery. I had to go out of my way to find this solution; more importantly, I suppose, I needed to believe that there might have been an Atlantis to begin with. The tangible evidence for a populated Atlantis seems so thin, or perhaps absent entirely, depending on your point of view, that the search for such a solution would never be undertaken at all without foresight and motivation to solve a puzzle that could have been a fool's errand. Even if one decides that there might have been such an extraordinary island in the Atlantic, one would have to look past the obvious approaches, which would lead to dead ends. I went down those roads first and came to the same dead ends. But I had a sense that there were clues that seemed to point to some logical route beyond.

It wasn't until several years after my initial attempts to find a working hypothesis that I stumbled upon some apparently unrelated research findings that filled in some of the gaps that had previously prevented me from seeing my way through to a successful end. I realized that if one only calculates the amount that the MAR is able to rise and fall based on the forces imparted by isostasy, one would come away with the same small numbers that I got in my first calculations that made it seem there wouldn't be enough rise to create a substantial island. But I was able to see there were other forces involved that contributed far more than those responsible for keeping a cork floating in water (i.e., isostasy). It seems to me that you must go out of your way to recognize the chain of events that leads to unleashing the forces that eventually create the impetus to raise the MAR as high as it is capable of rising.

Despite the fact that I'm using estimates only of the resultant forces involved in creating and destroying a large Atlantic island, there is so much force involved that any estimate using my back-of-the-envelope approach would enable a sizable island to appear during the proper time and place that Plato so emphatically insisted on: eleven thousand years ago.

In the next chapter, I will delve into what I believe the MAR was like at a point when it was above sea level. Judging by its location in the Atlantic, one can extrapolate the kind of weather that animals and plants might have enjoyed and what form of landscape one would have encountered.

CHAPTER 9
TIME MACHINE TO
AN ANTEDILUVIAN WORLD

It seems a bit odd writing about what it would be like to visit a place that's clearly hypothetical. What I've attempted to do, once again, is to use some best-fit, educated guesses about what Atlantis was like in terms of climate, terrain, and flora and fauna.

Let's start with what the island might have looked like during its tenure above the waves in the middle of the Pleistocene.

One thing I didn't mention previously about the raised MAR was that during the last ice age, when glaciers covered Iceland and the ridge would have been above sea level, the northern parts of it may have been covered with ice too. So, there might have been a land bridge of sorts connecting the northern parts of the raised MAR and Iceland. The bridge may have been merely an icy isthmus, but it was a connection nevertheless. I make this speculation because Plato claimed that all manner of animals inhabited Atlantis, and my first thought was to wonder how they would have gotten there. If the northern parts of the MAR were elevated enough, perhaps there was a land bridge for animals, as well as people, to travel along. As they progressively traveled more and more to the south (actually, the only direction they could on the long north-to-south-oriented island), they would have encountered an increasingly moderate climate.

The island we've constructed from the lowering of the sea level, isostatic rebound, and convection of magma from the diverted hot spot under

Iceland was situated at a convenient point in the Atlantic Ocean (see figure 36).

Figure 36. *Bathymetric view of the MAR (from NOAA satellite survey) in which the light-blue areas of the Azores Plateau depict a landmass that Plato's ancestors knew as the island of Atlantis. (Note: Greenland and Iceland appear larger than they should because of the map projection.)*

It's where the Gulf Stream current originating in the warm Caribbean becomes what is known as the North Atlantic Drift—it loops around the North Atlantic Ocean and would have passed the island Plato called Atlantis. As a result of this very same ocean current that is still part of a major gyre (circular ocean current) today, the Atlantic Ocean currents modify the climate of northern Scotland, rendering it mild enough that palm trees can flourish on its northwest coast.

It is interesting also that Plato described aspects of the island in detail, including naming a litany of plants that grew there. Among the types he mentions, he adds, "and the fruits having a hard rind, affording drinks and meats and ointments."

What he is describing could very easily be assumed to be coconuts. Coconuts are the fruit of palm trees, leading me to believe that perhaps he was insinuating that the climate of Atlantis was, at least, semitropical.

So, one might expect that being in a more southerly location than Scotland, the great Atlantic island of Atlantis might have benefited from this climatological twist. Now, Atlantis was really an archipelago, or a chain of islands. The main island, the one we've been talking about for a hundred pages or so, is the largest of the chain. It stretched, as far as I can tell, for anywhere from one thousand to fifteen hundred miles, north to south. This is one of the reasons why I believe Plato described it as having an extent equal to Libya and Asia.

Up and down the coast of this great island chain, the climate may have very well been comparable to that of southern Spain or even North Africa. It would be hard to know for sure, since having a large landmass near the middle of the Atlantic has never been part of any historical record, nor of any climate simulation. What I'm saying about the climate of this hypothetical island is, of course, highly speculative, but I think it's of interest to contemplate. Furthermore, there is good reason to believe that this would have been the same ocean flow, since this is the case today, and as far as we know, the currents haven't changed much since the last ice age. During the ice age, the Caribbean was still warm and never burdened by the glaciers' Arctic-like weather, so it still could have produced the same tropically heated water currents along the western coast of the island of Atlantis.

Before going too far, I should add that a large landmass in the Atlantic could very well have created a situation that produced quite different climatological results. But this would be an even greater hypothetical for which I would be contemplating an explanation. My original mission was to show that a large island once existed in the mid-Atlantic Ocean—and I believe I've made a convincing argument. *Proof* of a specific climate condition is a bridge too far.

While the glaciers were inexorably grinding forward with a relentless advance southward in the northern reaches of Europe and North America, Atlantis may have been a warm refuge for any flora or fauna landing on it. So, for any human finding the island of Atlantis, they would have also found a refuge not only from the frigid clime of the ice age but also from the hectic scramble to find and hold the scarce resources available in the Northern Hemisphere during this ice-blanketed time. Being on an island would have provided a significant advantage to those initial inhabitants. It would have been a microcosm of the wonders akin to those that were presented to the first humans entering North America. This new virgin land was unfettered by the competition of other humans—a land to do with and exploit as they pleased. Of course, that would be contingent on whether there were enough flora and fauna resources readily available for exploitation.

If we chose to compare what happens to newly emergent volcanic islands as flora and fauna attempt to gain a foothold, we need only to look around the world at other examples of similarly occurring geological and environmental events. A substantial volcanic island can transition from a barren, rocky terrain to a lush forest in a process called primary succession. These volcanic islands can form from several types of geologic and climatic events. Oceanic crust can be raised by a magma dome forming beneath it or by subsequent eruptions of a volcano finding a weak spot in the crust and building a mountain that rises above sea level. Due to the events we've discussed here, the sea level itself can drop and expose high points in the seafloor.

Whatever the case, what we see is that the rapidity at which volcanic islands become inhabited by plants and animals varies according to the degree and speed at which erosion occurs. Erosion is what creates the soil into which plants can sink their roots and obtain the nutrients they require to grow. Rain and wind grind away at rock, creating the familiar texture of soil. The addition of dead plant and animal matter further increases the nutrient value of this newly formed soil.

Depending on the climatic conditions, such as rainfall and temperature changes, volcanic rock can break down at different rates and different actions.

Some things can grow on rock such as Lichen and they are a part of the erosion cycle, but flowering plants generally cannot unless the rock is porous. Volcanic rock is porous and some plants can put roots in it. Plants capable of rooting into volcanic rock and accelerate the erosion process also.

Then there is the affect of rain and big swings in temperature range—causing rock to crack with heat or the expansion of frozen water that seeps into the tiny crevices. Most of the lower creatures of the food chain need plants to survive, and predators need them. Most animals need plants at some point in the food chain. Proximity to an established forest or jungle is important as a source of nutrients such as seeds, leaves and bark for immigrant animals. The bottom line is that, according to the US Geological Survey (1999), "A forest can develop in wet regions [of new volcanic islands] in less than 150 years."

It's clear, then, that not long after the large island of Atlantis was above the waves, life may very well have begun to establish itself on its rocky shores. My estimate is that this would have been as early as two hundred thousand years ago, when the last ice age was well underway—lowering the oceans and creating the initial isostatic uplifting. Once any life, such as lichen, got a foothold, a profusion of other flora would quickly follow. This was a time in which modern humans and Neanderthals occupied Europe together and, according to Neumann (2004), fire would likely have been a recent invention—and was used extensively by hominids. So, by the time the island had formed an ecological niche for life, humans stumbling upon it in search of the scarce ice age resources would already have brought with them the new technology of fire.

Getting to the Atlantic island would have been a task during the last ice age. The land or ice bridge concept would have been the most likely in my opinion. But traveling over the intervening ocean would have presented unique obstacles. Traveling to Atlantis from the coast of Europe would have been a trip of about six hundred miles due west of Lisbon.

As arduous as that journey may seem humans have covered much greater distance over water with only the most primitive sailing vessels. So, a journey of 600 hundred miles from the Iberian coast to the raised MAR might appear doable compared to the near-impossible challenges of voyages of many thousands of miles taken by the Polynesians of a thousand years ago through the open waters of the Pacific.

If we submit that the *Homo sapiens* and Neanderthals of the ice age may have been able to surmount the trip, although no evidence exists (even though, as late as eleven thousand years ago in Europe, these peoples were able to build or use boats to sail the open sea), world-renowned linguist Dr. Daniel Everett (2017) speculated that *Homo erectus* was able to navigate the open waters of the Indonesian island of Flores in the Pacific in part because they had developed language, enabling them to organize the voyage to the isolated island on which the first fossils of their existence were found. This is a hominid that was clearly not as sophisticated as *Homo sapiens* but was able to sail the open sea. So, it is possible that the more sophisticated inhabitants of Pleistocene Europe may have been able to construct simple rafts to make it to the island of Atlantis. It's the setting for many a tale—of people sailing near the shore, being swept out to sea by strong currents, and finding uncharted islands. But, then again, there is still the strong possibility that the northern reaches of the Atlantean island were connected by a thin land or ice bridge, which would have enabled animals as well as humans to reach the island without having first developed any sailing technology.

Despite any speculative question concerning this hypothetical island, it was unknown until recently that the peoples of Gobekli Tepe who existed eleven thousand years ago were able to construct monoliths carved with animal depictions far more sophisticated than Stonehenge, which dates back *only* forty-five hundred years. Maybe those living along the western coast of Europe were smart enough to conceive of and build simple sea-faring boats or rafts, even though we've found no evidence of them. And doesn't the technology of the *Kon-Tiki* voyages seem less challenging than that of designing massive monoliths, or stone carvings, and then hauling and erecting them, all of which took place eleven thousand years ago at the Gobekli Tepe site in modern-day Turkey?

The landscape encountered by those stepping onto the shores of Atlantis would have been very much as depicted by Plato. In the *Critias* he says of the landscape, "The whole country was said by him to be very lofty and precipitous on the side of the sea." The incline of the seafloor around the MAR is in fact steep, perhaps owing to its bulging of the normally flat seafloor.

The appearance of a large island at the point above the present MAR may very well have changed the ocean currents that flow there today. That would undoubtedly have had some effect on the local climate. We will see later that the Atlantic currents can create stark differences in weather patterns in adjacent geographical locations, such that palm trees grow next to regions that are blanketed with snow.

Those making it to Atlantis would have found it a safe place from the turmoil of mainland Europe, where clans of humans were at odds with each other over hunting and foraging resources. Those arriving on the island would have found something novel—Atlantis was, like its kindred spirit, Iceland, a land of hot springs. The hot springs still exist in the Azores today, and interestingly enough, Plato described the abundance of springs, both cold and hot, as follows:

In the next place, they had fountains, one of cold and another of hot water, in gracious plenty flowing; and they were wonderfully adapted for use by reason of the pleasantness and excellence of their waters. They constructed buildings about them and planted suitable trees, also they made cisterns, some open to the heavens, others roofed over, to be used in winter as warm baths; there were kings' baths, and the baths of private persons, which were kept apart; and there were separated baths for women, and for horses, and to each of them they gave as much adornment as was suitable.

Plato believed that Atlantis was a place with many hot springs, and he spent a great deal of time describing them in his dialogues. The reason I bring this up is that there would undoubtedly have been many hot springs dotted all along the island, just as we find in Iceland and the Azores today. And there is a reason for that. The hot magma propping up the island, as in Iceland, comes in contact with the water tables, preheating the water, at times to the point of creating geysers.

Plato described the Atlantean kingdom in considerable detail. Undoubtedly the most memorable for those closely following the myth is his claim that the central metropolis of Atlantis was constructed in the form of concentric circular canals. The canals were set on a large plain that was surrounded by a circular mountain range. The circular canals were divided into quadrants by radial canals that afforded a means for boats to navigate from the center of the metropolis to the concentric rings and out to the nearby sea.

In figure 37, a bathymetric map of the MAR (with an outline of the proposed Atlantis shoreline) includes an insert depicting a large circular mountain range—probably an extinct volcanic caldera that encircles a great plain that itself terminates at the edge of what would have been a shoreline, if the island were above sea level. This is what Plato said about the circular appearance of the Atlantean central city:

I have described the city and the environs of the ancient palace nearly in the words of Solon, and now I must endeavour to represent the nature and arrangement of the rest of the land. The whole country was said by him to be very lofty and precipitous on the side of the sea, but the country immediately about and surrounding the city was a level plain, itself surrounded by mountains which descended towards the sea; it was smooth and even, and of an oblong shape, extending in one direction three thousand stadia, but across the centre inland it was two thousand stadia. This part of the island looked towards the south and was sheltered from the north. The surrounding mountains were celebrated for their number and size and beauty, far beyond any which still exist, having in them also many wealthy villages of country folk, and rivers, and lakes, and meadows supplying food enough for every animal, wild or tame, and much wood of various sorts, abundant for each and every kind of work.

I will now describe the plain, as it was fashioned by nature and by the labours of many generations of kings through long ages. It was for the most part rectangular and oblong, and where falling out of the straight line followed the circular ditch. The depth, and width, and length of this ditch were incredible, and gave the impression that a work of such extent, in addition to so many others, could never have been artificial. Nevertheless I must say what I was told. It was excavated to the depth of a hundred feet, and its breadth was a stadium everywhere; it was carried round the whole of the plain, and was ten thousand stadia in length. It received the streams which came down from the mountains, and winding round the plain and meeting at the city, was there let off into the sea. Farther inland, likewise, straight canals of a hundred feet in width were cut from it through the plain, and again let off into the ditch leading to the sea: these canals were at intervals of a hundred stadia, and by them they brought down the wood from the mountains to the city, and conveyed the fruits of the earth in ships, cutting transverse passages from one canal into another, and to the city. Twice in the year they gathered the fruits of the earth—in winter having the benefit of the rains of heaven, and in summer the water which the land supplied by introducing streams from the canals.

Figure 37. Geologic formations of a circular mountain range in the insert bear a strong resemblance to Plato's account of where the Atlanteans established their kingdom, with access to the nearby sea.

As the island was lifted, or, from another point of view, inflated like a balloon, the thin oceanic crust would have been stretched. The stretching produces cracks in the crust into which seawater is infused. The seawater is heated and, under pressure, forced out of cracks at higher elevations along the incline of the raised ridge as smoky effluent (which is the origin of the term "black smokers"). Because the oceanic crust is so much thinner than the crust of, say, Iceland, it should be expected to react more dramatically to the pressures of the percolated seawater that infused into the crust all along the MAR. What we see is a picture of the stretched crust, riddled with stretch cracks and letting in seawater heated by the rising magma and then "inflating" as the sea levels drop, with migrating magma pouring in below. The entire extent of any island would have been undermined by the stresses created by the magma, hot seawater, and steam. The hot springs would be sources of highly mineralized water.

As an aside to the interesting and speculative, I'll mention that Plato talked of the peoples of Atlantis becoming hostile and aggressive, often attacking the inhabitants of the Mediterranean basin. In a final chapter on Atlantis, Plato told of a monumental battle between those outside forces and the defenders of the Mediterranean: "But afterwards there occurred violent earthquakes and floods; and in a single day and night of misfortune all your warlike men in a body sank into the earth, and the island of Atlantis in like manner disappeared in the depths of the sea."

After many centuries of life on the Atlantean island, the inhabitants may very well have become aware of an unnerving process—their land was sinking. In the last period of Atlantean habitation, they would have become keenly aware that the shorelines were increasingly being lost to the ever-rising levels of the sea. This unsettling trend could have led to the Atlanteans seeking to expand their territory against the threat of the oceans swallowing the land they had relied on for centuries. Their encroachment into the territory of the inhabitants of Europe could have sparked the hostile interaction that eventually led to the wars that Plato claimed ensued and ended with the cataclysm that is at the root of the story of Atlantis. The final demise by earthquakes and inundations could have led to the dark period where the existence of the Atlantean island was lost in the depths of destruction caused by the wars and natural disasters that had befallen the inhabitants of the Mediterranean basin.

I'll end by stating that the Atlantis myth has endured for centuries in Western culture, more than any other such legendary story. A 2017 Chapman University survey found that 55 percent of those surveyed believe in the likelihood of the existence of this lost ice age civilization (Colavito 2017). That is not the reason I set out to write this book, but it does point to the compelling story it represents and its enduring influence on our civilization, whether it turns out to be true or not. I hope I have moved the discussion far enough forward that further examination of what I've presented becomes the source of a fresh look at this monumental story.

APPENDIX

For those interested in a more robust explanation of the quantitative aspects of the book's premise, this appendix should serve to satisfy that interest. My contention that the Mid-Atlantic Ridge could rise thousands of feet to produce a large island might sound absurd, but the following presentation will show that it's not far-fetched at all.

First, I notice that there is a great disparity between the depth of the ocean basins and the MAR. This disparity is caused by the different forces under each region of the ocean floor. I calculated the difference between the purely isostatic uplift force under the basins away from the ridge and the spreading center convection current force under the MAR. While the weight of the oceans can push down the seafloor that lies away from the spreading center to as much as 17,500 feet on either side of the ridge, it is only able to push the MAR around the Azores down to about 6,000 feet, where, as noted previously, there are some islands above sea level. I notice the fractional difference between the isostatic versus the mid-oceanic plume forces is the depth of the ocean basin divided by the depth of the MAR. Overall seabed subsidence divided by subsidence at the MAR, as follows:

17,500 feet/6,000 feet = 2.92 or nearly 3

Therefore, the force of the spreading center current under the MAR provides three times the uplift force as the isostatic forces under the rest of the ocean floors. Next, I calculate what this disparity looked like during the Pleistocene.

There was substantially lower sea level during the Pleistocene. The Middleton/Wilcock rule states the glaciers push down the land 1/3 of their height. By the same reasoning, we could say that because the last ice age lowered sea levels by about 420 feet, the isostatic rebound of the seafloor should have been approximately a third of the depth of seawater that was removed, which amounts to a rise of about 140 feet.

Now I factor in that the spreading center currents under the MAR provide three times the uplift force under the rest of the ocean bottom, and I multiply the normal rise due to sea-level drop by three. If the sea-bed normally would rise 140 feet, then the MAR should rise three times that amount.

140 feet × 3 = 420 feet

We also need to add the amount that the sea level dropped, which was 420 feet. The result becomes 420 feet + 420 feet = 840 feet of apparent rise for the MAR. But even 840 feet isn't nearly enough to make a big island at the MAR. The size of the island will be proportional to the amount of sea level lowering. To visualize the of the island that fulfills the target size I use a bathymetric map, in which isobars represent imaginary shorelines. The one most near the description presented by Plato requires a sea level drop of at least 6,500 feet (see figure 23 in Chapter 7). It's clear that an 840-foot drop does not produce a sufficiently large island outline. I need to show another process that will add uplift.

During the last ice age, glaciers reached 5,850 feet, or 1,800 meters, on Iceland, causing the central plain to sink 1,625 feet, or 500 meters, under that weight, according to Sigmundsson (2006). Not only did they push the central plain down, but they diverted the hot spot plume away from Iceland.

Figure 20 in chapter 6 vividly portrays the evidence that the hot spot plume migrated south, away from the Icelandic Plateau. Figure 27 in chapter 7 shows the glacial distribution on the Icelandic Plateau during and after the ice age. Note that after the ice age, as the glaciers melted down, only the thickest remain today, over the southeastern, central plain.

Figure 21 shows the coincidence of the major ice pack and hot spot on the Icelandic Plateau leaving no doubt the flow of the plume was subject to the presence of the glaciers. According to Vink (1985), the plume could be diverted toward the spreading center, south of the Icelandic Plateau. The infusion of magma to the MAR could create the additional uplift I'm looking for.

I need to calculate how much magma could be diverted and end up under the Azores Plateau region of the MAR and how much uplift it could produce. There are estimates of the magma flow under Iceland, but I find I need the resultant uplift they create more than the volume. Figure 25 in chapter 7 depicts the downward force of the glaciers on the central plain of Iceland. I calculate the approximate area of the plain. I know that when the plume was allowed to return to the central plain, the crust was uplifted 1,625 feet. I have to calculate how much uplift that Icelandic magma, being diverted to an area under the MAR, will produce. I find that the crusts of the Icelandic Plateau and the Azores Plateau have different thicknesses. And that the two crusts are supported differently. I see that these conditions have to be taken into account to find the amount of new uplift.

I can visualize the individual crusts as types of structural beams and model a process from that. The Icelandic Plateau crust could be represented as a structure type called the simple beam. This type of beam is fixed at both ends, whereas the MAR is more or less a cantilever beam. This type of beam is attached at one end and the other is free to flap.

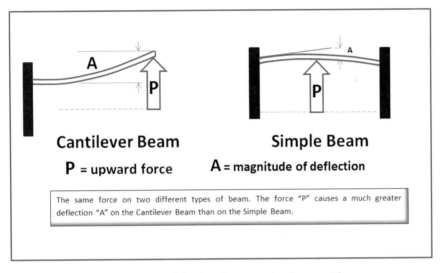

Figure 1-A. Beam deflection diagram—simple vs. cantilever.

The structure of the MAR is represented by two such cantilever beams facing each other. The diagram in figure 1-A demonstrates a qualitative relationship between simple and cantilever beam types. A quantitative representation of each beam is also depicted. The cantilever beam equation is as follows:

$$\delta = \frac{PL^3}{3YI}$$

Where:

δ = magnitude of deflection

P = the load

L = beam length

I = moment of inertia

Y = Young's modulus

This second equation is for the simple beam:

$$\delta = \frac{PL^3}{48YI}$$

What can be said about these two equations that would help us understand how they produce different degrees of uplift? They are identical, except for the constant factor in the denominator. The larger denominator of the simple beam indicates it will produce a smaller deflection per unit force than the cantilever beam. Just as 1/4 is smaller than 1/2, 1/48 is smaller than 1/3. In fact, the cantilever beam produces sixteen times greater deflection than the simple beam per unit force.

We have to conclude that when the magma from Iceland arrived under the Azores Plateau, it should produce sixteen times the uplift—all other things being equal. But not only is the MAR crust easier to uplift because it is cantilevered, it is also thinner.

The crust of Iceland is about twenty-nine kilometers thick. The crust of the Azores Plateau is about fifteen kilometers thick. There is a crust thickness difference of about 2:1. This phenomenon of flexibility as a function of material and material thickness is called flexural rigidity. Flexural rigidity is defined as the resistance of a beam or plate to a bending deformation. The equation follows:

$$D = \frac{Eh^3}{12(1 - v^2)}$$

Where

D = flexural rigidity—resistance to bending

E = Young's modulus—force to stretch a beam*

h = thickness of the beam

v = Poisson's ratio—elastic change in shape*

(Note: the * indicates simplifications of material phenomenon.)

If all the factors remain the same, that is, if we compare similar crust material, the only difference will be in the value of h in the equation representing crust thickness. Looking at the equation we can see that D is directly proportional to h^3. If $h = 2$, then $D = 8$; if $h = 4$, then $D = 64$. It is clear that a small decrease in thickness produces a very large increase in flexibility.

Since the Icelandic Plateau is two times the thickness of the MAR, it should be obvious that the crust of the MAR will be eight times more flexible. Combined with the factor of sixteen times greater deflection due to the cantilever nature of the MAR, I'm predicting a very large uplift, so far.

It looks like there will be a significant difference in the ability of the diverted magma to uplift crust solely depending on where it ends up. However, before going any further, some readers might have noticed that there are two issues not addressed.

First, the two cantilever beams facing each other are not completely free to move because at the point that they meet, the ends of the cantilevered crusts are tenuously held together by the magmatic rock. I found that Vishal et al. (2011) studied the strength of semi-molten rock. They reported that rock loses 70 percent of its tensile strength at 250 The tensile strength is a measure of the material to resist the stress of stretching before breaking. This will show the degree the weakly joined ends of the spreading center crust will resist uplift. In developing this calculation, I decided to use a conservative value of 50 percent in my calculation of the temperature dependent flexibility-damping of the crust, because the temperature of the rock at the spreading centers can vary.

Because of the temperature effect on the ability of the crustal rock to be free to move, I reduced by 50 percent the result of the beam disparity, which is 16-fold, and the 8-fold rise differential due to flexural rigidity:

$(16 \times .5) \times (8 \times .5)$

or

$8 \times 4 = 32$-fold rise.

The second issue not addressed in these calculations is the area disparity. The area of the new island, according to my mapping on Google Earth, is about 141,000 square miles, compared to the central plain in Iceland that was depressed, which was about 20,000 square miles. The new island will have an area about seven times the corresponding region of the Icelandic Plateau.

$141,000/20,000 \approx 7.1$, and then divided the combined beam and flexure disparity by that:

$32/7.1 \approx 4.5$-fold rise.

If all the parameters that we've discussed are taken into account in one expression, we can write an equation that approximates the amount that the MAR could have been uplifted by the divergent Icelandic magma plume and the lowering of sea level. That equation should look like the one below:

Where:

R_1 = rise from lowered sea level (1/3 glacial rebound × 3 height disparity of the MAR)

C_B = cantilevered versus simple beam multiplier ($16 \times .50 = 8x$)

F_R = flexural rigidity difference by thickness $29/15 \approx 2$, $2^3 = 8$, $8 \times .50 = 4$

R_2 = glacial rebound of Icelandic Plateau (+1,625)

A = area differential between Iceland and the MAR (1:7.1) Area disparity 141k/20k = 7.1

Substituting values into the equation, we get the following:

420 feet + ((8 × 4 × 1,625 feet)/7.1)) ≈ 7,743-foot rise

This is a little bit more than I had originally calculated; however, it is clear that it is within the range that shows the displaced magma from

Iceland could easily have uplifted the MAR around the Azores Plateau, high enough to create the large island that is depicted by Plato in his dialogues.

REFERENCES

Agassiz, Louis. 1840. *Étude sur les Glaciers*. Neuchâtel, SW: Jent et Gassmann.

Ahlbom, Kaj, Timo Äikäs, and Lars O. Ericsson. 1991. *SKB/TVO Ice Age Scenario*. SKB Technical Report 91–32. Stockholm: Swedish Nuclear Fuel and Waste Management.

Allen, Richard M., Guust Nolet, W. Jason Morgan, Kristín Vogfjörd, Meredith Nettles, Göran Ekström, Bergur H. Bergsson, Pálmi Erlendsson, G. R. Foulger, Steinunn Jakobsdóttir, Bruce R. Julian, Matt Pritchard, Sturla Ragnarsson, and Ragnar Stefánsson. 2002. "Plume-Driven Plumbing and Crustal Formation in Iceland." *Journal of Geophysical Research* 107 (B8): ESE 4-1–ESE 4-19. doi:10.1029/2001JB000584.

Artyushkov, Eugene V., and Albrecht W. Hofmann. 1998. "Neotectonic Crustal Uplift on the Continents and Its Possible Mechanisms: The Case of Southern Africa." *Surveys in Geophysics* 19: 369–415.

Banks, R. J., R. L. Parker, and S. P. Huestis. 1977. "Isostatic Compensation on a Continental Scale: Local versus Regional Mechanisms." *Geophysical Journal International* 51 (2): 431–52.

Benediktsdóttir, A., R. N. Hey, F. Martinez, and A. Höskuldsson. 2011. "Detailed Tectonic Evolution of the Reykjanes Ridge during the

Past 15 Ma." *Geochemistry, Geophysics, Geosystems* 13 (2). doi:10.1029/2011GC003948.

Biello, David. 2012. "What Thawed the Last Ice Age?" *Scientific American.* April 4, 2012. https://www.scientificamerican.com/article/ what-thawed-the-last-ice-age.

Biessy, G., O. Dauteuil, B. Van Vliet-Lanoë, and A. Wayolle. 2008. "Fast and Partitioned Postglacial Rebound of Southwestern Iceland." *Tectonics* 27 (3). doi:10.1029/2007TC002177.

Björck, Svante. 2013. "Younger Dryas Oscillation, Global Evidence." In *Encyclopedia of Quaternary Science, Vol. 3*, edited by Scotty A. Elias, 1987–94. Amsterdam: Elsevier.

Boschi, Lapo, Jeroen Tromp, and Richard J. O'Connell. 1999. "On Maxwell Singularities in Postglacial Rebound." *Geophysical Journal International* 136 (2): 492–98.

Bottinga Y., and D. F. Weill. 1970. "Densities of Liquid Silicate Systems Calculated from Partial Molar Volumes of Oxide Components." *American Journal of Science* 269 (2): 169–82.

Carlson, A. E. 2013. "The Younger Dryas Climate Event." In *Encyclopedia of Quaternary Science, Vol. 3*, edited by Scotty A. Elias, 126–34. Amsterdam: Elsevier.

Christensen, Ulrich R. 1985. "Mantle Phase Transitions and Postglacial Rebound." *Journal of Geophysical Research* 90 (B13): 11,312–18.

Colavito, Jason. 2017. "Chapman University Survey Finds Majority of Americans Now Believe in Ancient Advanced Civilization, while a

Third Believe in Ancient Astronauts." *Jason Colavito* (blog). October 14, 2017. http://www.jasoncolavito.com/blog/chapman-university-survey-finds-majority-of-americans-now-believe-in-ancient-advanced-civilization-while-a-third-believe-in-ancient-astronauts.

Dietrich, Oliver, Klaus Schmidt, Çiğdem Köksal-Schmidt, and Jens Notroff. 2013. "Establishing a Radiocarbon Sequence for Göbekli Tepe: State of Research and New Data." *Neo-Lithics* 1: 36–47.

Donnelly, Ignatius L. 1882. *Atlantis: The Antediluvian World*. New York: Harper & Brothers.

Drye, Willie. n.d. "Atlantis Legend." *National Geographic*. Accessed March 9, 2020. https://www.nationalgeographic.com/history/archaeology/atlantis.

Engel, A. E. J., and C. G. Engel. 1970. *Igneous Rocks Recovered on Leg 2: Initial Reports of the Deep Sea Drilling Project, Vol. 2*. Washington, DC: US Government Printing Office.

Ewing, Maurice, Bruce C. Heezen, D. B. Erickson, John Northrop, and James Dorman. *1953*. *"Exploration of the Northwest Atlantic Mid-Ocean Canyon."* *GSA Bulletin* 64 (7): 865–68.

Ewing, Maurice, David Bukry, J. Lamar Worzel, Arthur O. Beall, and William A. Berggren. 1969. *Initial Reports of the Deep Sea Drilling Project, Vol. 1*. Washington, DC: National Science Foundation.

Everett, Daniel L. 2017. *How Language Began: The Story of Humanity's Greatest Invention*. New York: Liveright.

Fairbanks, R. G. 1989. "A 17,000-Year Glacio-Eustatic Sea Level Record: Influence of Glacial Melting on the Younger Dryas Event and Deep-Ocean Circulation." *Nature* 342: 637–42.

Fischer, Irene. 1975. "Another Look at Eratosthenes' and Posidonius' Determinations of the Earth's Circumference." *Quarterly Journal of the Royal Astronomical Society* 16: 152–67.

Fjeldskaar, Willy. 1997. "Flexural Rigidity of Fennoscandia Inferred from the Postglacial Uplift." *Tectonics* 16 (4): 596–608.

Forsstrom, Lars. 1999. *Future Glaciation in Fennoscandia*. Helsinki, FI: Posiva Oy.

Forte, A. M., W. R. Peltier, A. M. Dziewonski, and R. L. Woodward. 1993. "Dynamic Surface Topography: A New Interpretation Based upon Mantle Flow Models Derived from Seismic Tomography." *Geophysical Research Letters* 20 (3): 225–28.

Foulger, Gillian R. 2010. *Plates vs. Plumes: A Geological Controversy*. Oxford, UK: Wiley-Blackwell.

Fowler, C. M. R. 2005. *The Solid Earth: An Introduction to Global Geophysics*. 2nd ed. Cambridge: Cambridge University Press.

Federico Pasquaré Mariotto andFabio Luca Bonali. *Virtual Geosites as Innovative Tools for Geoheritage. Geosciences 2021, 11(4), 149; https:// www.mdpi.com/2076-3263/11/4/149*

Frederikse, Thomas, Riccardo E. M. Riva, and Matt A. King. 2017. "Ocean Bottom Deformation due to Present-Day Mass Redistribution and

Its Impact on Sea Level Observations." *Geophysical Research Letters* 44: 12306–314.

Freely, John. 2013. *Before Galileo: The Birth of Modern Science in Medieval Europe.* New York: Overlook Duckworth, Peter Mayer Publishers.

Garai, Jozsef. 2003. "Post Glacial Rebounds Measure the Viscosity of the Lithosphere." https://arxiv.org/pdf/physics/0308002.pdf.

Georgen, Jennifer E., and Ravi D. Sankar. 2020. "Effects of Ridge Geometry on Mantle Dynamics in an Oceanic Triple Junction Region: Implications for the Azores Plateau." *Earth and Planetary Science Letters* 298 (1–2): 23–34.

Gow, Mary. 2010. *Measuring the Earth: Eratosthenes and His Celestial Geometry.* Berkeley Heights, NJ: Enslow.

Hall, N., and T. Krupa. 2006. "The New England Seamount Chain." *The Traprock* 6: 9–13.

Hékinian, Roger. 1984. "Undersea Volcanoes." *Scientific American* 251 (1): 46–55.

Ingólfsson, Ólafur. n.d. "Icelandic Glaciers." Accessed March 9, 2020. https://notendur.hi.is/oi/icelandic_glaciers.htm.

Intergovernmental Committee on Surveying and Mapping. n.d. "History of Mapping." Accessed March 9, 2020. https://www.icsm.gov.au/education/fundamentals-mapping/history-mapping.

Iowa State University. 2011. "Beam Deflection Formulae." September 25, 2011. http://home.eng.iastate.edu/~shermanp/STAT447/STAT%20 Articles/Beam_Deflection_Formulae.pdf.

Jean-Baptiste, P., P. Allard, R. Coutinho, T. Ferreira, E. Fourré, G. Queiroz, and J. L. Gaspar. 2009. "Helium Isotopes in Hydrothermal Volcanic Fluids of the Azores Archipelago." *Earth and Planetary Science Letters* 281 (1–2): 70–80.

Jull, M., and D. McKenzie. 1996. "The Effect of Deglaciation on Mantle Melting beneath Iceland." *Journal of Geophysical Research* 101 (B10): 21815–828.

Larson, Kristine M., and Tonie van Dam. 2000. "Measuring Postglacial Rebound with GPS and Absolute Gravity." *Geophysical Research Letters* 27 (23): 3925–28.

Lowrie, William. 2004. *Fundamentals of Geophysics. Cambridge: Cambridge University Press.*

Lunkka, Juha P. 2011. "Scandinavian Glaciers." In *Encyclopedia of Snow, Ice, and Glaciers*, edited by Vijay P. Singh, Pratap Singh, and Umesh K. Haritashya. Encyclopedia of Earth Sciences Series. Dordrecht, NL: Springer Dordrecht.

Macdonald, Ken C., and Bruce Luyendyk. 1981. "The Crest of the East Pacific Rise." *Scientific American* 244 (5): 100–17.

Malmberg, Svend-Aage. 2004. *The Iceland Basin: Topography and Oceanographic Features.* Reykjavik, Iceland: Marine Research Institute.

Middleton, Gerard V., and Peter R. Wilcock. 1994. *Mechanics in the Earth and Environmental Sciences.* Cambridge: Cambridge University Press.

Muller, Richard A., and Gordon J. MacDonald. 1997. "Glacial Cycles and Astronomical Forcing." *Science* 277 (5323): 215–18.

National Oceanic and Atmospheric Administration. n.d. "Glacial-Interglacial Cycles." Accessed March 9, 2020. https://www.ncdc.noaa.gov/abrupt-climate-change/Glacial-Interglacial%20Cycles.

National Oceanic and Atmospheric Administration. 2018. "How Deep Is the Ocean?" Last updated June 25, 2018. http://oceanservice.noaa.gov/facts/oceandepth.html.

Neumann, Nadja. 2004. "Earliest Fire Sheds Light on Hominids." *Nature.* doi:10.1038/news040426-16.

Payne, Robert. 1959. *The Gold of Troy: The Story of Heinrich Schliemann and the Buried Cities of Ancient Greece.* New York: Funk & Wagnalls.

PhysOrg.com. 2009. "The Impact of Sea-Level Rise on Atmospheric CO2 Concentrations."http://phys.org/news/2009-01-impact-sea-level-atmospheric-co2.html.

Plato. (1871). *The Dialogues of Plato, Vol. 3.* Translated by Benjamin Jowett. Oxford: Oxford University Press.

Prothero, Donald R., and Fred Schwab. 1996. *Sedimentary Geology: An Introduction to Sedimentary Rocks and Stratigraphy.* 2nd ed. New York: W. H. Freeman and Company.

Quartau, Rui. 2007. "The Insular Shelf of Faial: Morphological and Sedimentary Evolution." PhD diss., Universidade de Aveiro, Spain.

Radford, Benjamin. 2018. "'Lost' City of Atlantis: Fact and Fable." https://www.livescience.com/23217-lost-city-of-atlantis.html.

Reynolds, Hannah I., Magnús T. Gudmundsson, and Thórdís Högnadóttir. 2015. "Subglacial Melting Associated with Activity at Bárdarbunga Volcano, Iceland, Explored Using Numerical Reservoir Simulations." Paper presented at the EGU General Assembly, Vienna, Austria, April 2015.

Rohling, Eelco J., Ivan D. Haigh, Gavin L. Foster, Andrew P. Roberts, and Katharine M. Grant. 2013. "A Geological Perspective on Potential Future Sea-Level Rise." *Scientific Reports* 3 (3461). doi:10.1038/srep03461.

Rohling, E. J., M. Fenton, F. J. Jorissen, P. Bertrand, G. Ganssen, and J. P. Caulet. 1998. "Magnitudes of Sea-Level Lowstands of the Past 500,000 Years." *Nature* 394: 162–65.

Rose, Mark. 1998. "First Mariners." *Archeology* 51 (3).

Rusli, N., M. R. Majid, and A. H. M. Din. 2014. "Google Earth's Derived Digital Elevation Model: A Comparative Assessment with Aster and SRTM Data." Paper presented at the 8th International Symposium of the Digital Earth, Sarawak, Malaysia, August 2014.

Sandwell, D. T., S. T. Gille, and W. H. F. Smith. 2002. "Bathymetry from Space: Oceanography, Geophysics, and Climate." Workshop presented at Geoscience Professional Services, Bethesda, MD, June 2002.

Scalera, Giancarlo. 2003. "Roberto Mantovani, an Italian Defender of the Continental Drift and Planetary Expansion." In *Why Expanding Earth? A Book in Honour of O. C. Hilgenberg*, edited by Giancarlo Scalera and Karl-Heinz Jacob, 71–74. Rome: INVG.

Schoch, Robert M. 2000. "Geological Evidence Pertaining to the Age of the Great Sphinx." Circular Times (website). http://www.robertschoch. net/Geological%20Evidence%20Sphinx%202000.htm.

Searle, R. C. 1976. "Lithospheric Structure of the Azores Plateau from Rayleigh-Wave Dispersion." *Geophysical Journal International* 44 (3): 537–46.

Settegast, Mary. 1990. *Plato, Prehistorian: 10,000 to 5,000 B.C.—Myth, Religion, and Archaeology*. Hudson, NY: Lindisfarne Press.

Sigmundsson, Freysteinn. 2006. *Iceland Geodynamics: Crustal Deformation and Divergent Plate Tectonics*. Chichester, UK: Praxis.

Sigurðsson, Einar Ragnar. 2013. "The Azores—A Triple Junction on a Hot Spot." April 11, 2013. https://notendur.hi.is/~ers12/skrar/Azores%20 TJ%20and%20HS_presentation_Einar%20Ragnar.pdf.

Singh, Satish C., Wayne C. Crawford, Hélène Carton, Tim Seher, Violaine Combier, Mathilde Cannat, Juan Pablo Canales, Doga Düsünür, Javier Escartin, and J. Miguel Miranda. 2006. "Discovery of a Magma Chamber and Faults beneath a Mid-Atlantic Ridge Hydrothermal Field." *Nature* 442: 1029–32.

Snir, Ainit, Dani Nadel, Iris Groman-Yaroslavski, Yoel Melamed, Marcelo Sternberg, Ofer Bar-Yosef, and Ehud Weiss. 2015. "The Origin of

Cultivation and Proto-Weeds, Long before Neolithic Farming." *PLOS ONE* 10 (7): e0131422. doi:10.1371/journal.pone.0131422.

Spieker, Kathrin, Stéphane Rondenay, Ricardo Ramalho, Christine Thomas, and George Helffrich. 2018. "Constraints on the Structure of the Crust and Lithosphere beneath the Azores Islands from Teleseismic Receiver Functions." *Geophysical Journal International* 213 (2): 824–35.

Thordarson, T., and G. Larsen. 2007. "Volcanism in Iceland in Historical Time: Volcano Types, Eruption Styles and Eruptive History." *Journal of Geodynamics* 43 (1): 118–52.

University of California Museum of Paleontology. 2011. "The Pleistocene Epoch." Last updated June 10, 2011. http://www.ucmp.berkeley.edu/ quaternary/pleistocene.php.

US Geological Survey. n.d. "Active Volcanoes of Hawaii." Accessed March 9, 2020. https://volcanoes.usgs.gov/observatories/hvo/hvo_volca-noes.html.

US Geological Survey. 1999. "Exploring the Deep Ocean Floor: Hot Springs and Strange Creatures." Last updated August 24, 1999. http://pubs. usgs.gov/gip/dynamic/exploring.html.

US Geological Survey. 2012. "Historical Perspective." Last updated August 7, 2012. http://pubs.usgs.gov/gip/dynamic/historical.html.

Verhoef, J., and B. J. Collette. 1987. "Lithospheric Thinning under the Atlantis-Meteor Seamount Complex (North Atlantic)." In *Seamounts, Islands, and Atolls*, edited by B. H. Keating, P. Fryer, R.

Batiza, and G. W. Boehlert, 391–405. Washington, DC: American Geophysical Union.

Vink, Gregory E., Jason Morgan, and Peter R. Vogt. 1985. "The Earth's Hot Spots." *Scientific American* 252 (4): 50–57.

Vishal, V., S. P. Pradhan, and T. N. Singh. 2011. "Tensile Strength of Rock Under Elevated Temperatures." *Geotechnical and Geological Engineering* 29 (6): 1127–33.

Walcott, R. I. 1970. "Flexural Rigidity, Thickness, and Viscosity of the Lithosphere." *Journal of Geophysical Research* 75 (20): 3941–54.

Watts, A. B., J. R. Cochran, and G. Selzer. 1975. "Gravity Anomalies and Flexure of the Lithosphere: A Three-Dimensional Study of the Great Meteor Seamount, Northeast Atlantic." *Journal of Geophysical Research* 80 (11): 1391–98. https://www.mdpi.com/2076-3263/11/4/149